TOTAL
MEDITATION

BESTSELLERS BY DEEPAK CHOPRA

Ageless Body, Timeless Mind

The Book of Secrets

Buddha: A Story of Enlightenment

God: A Story of Revelation

Grow Younger, Live Longer (with coauthor David Simon)

The Healing Self (with coauthor Rudolph E. Tanzi, PhD)

How to Know God

Jesus: A Story of Enlightenment

Life After Death

Metahuman

Muhammad: A Story of a Prophet

The Path to Love

Peace Is the Way

Perfect Health

Quantum Healing

Radical Beauty (with coauthor Kimberly Snyder, CN)

Reinventing the Body, Resurrecting the Soul

The Return of Merlin

The Seven Spiritual Laws of Success

The Shadow Effect (with coauthors Debbie Ford
and Marianne Williamson)

Spiritual Solutions

Super Brain (with coauthor Rudolph E. Tanzi, PhD)

Super Genes (with coauthor Rudolph E. Tanzi, PhD)

The Third Jesus

The 13th Disciple: A Spiritual Adventure

War of the Worldviews (with coauthor Leonard Mlodinow)

The Way of the Wizard

What Are You Hungry For?

You Are the Universe (with coauthor Menas C. Kafatos, PhD)

ALSO BY DEEPAK CHOPRA

The Angel Is Near

Ask Deepak about Death and Dying

Ask Deepak about Health

Ask Deepak about Love and Relationships

Ask Deepak about Meditation & Higher Consciousness

Ask Deepak about Spirituality

Ask Deepak about Success

Ask the Kabala (with coauthor Michael Zapolin)

Boundless Energy

Brain, Mind and Cosmos: The Nature of Our Existence and the Universe
(edited by Deepak Chopra with contributions
from notable scientists and philosophers)

Brotherhood: Dharma, Destiny, and the American Dream
(with coauthor Sanjiv Chopra)

The Chopra Center Cookbook (with coauthors David Simon
and Leanne Backer)

The Chopra Center Herbal Handbook (with coauthor David Simon)

Consciousness and the Universe (with coauthors Stuart Hameroff
and Sir Roger Penrose)

Creating Affluence

Creating Health

The Daughters of Joy

The Deeper Wound

TOTAL
MEDITATION

STRESS FREE LIVING
STARTS HERE

Deepak Chopra

I

Rider, an imprint of Ebury Publishing,
20 Vauxhall Bridge Road,
London SW1V 2SA

Rider is part of the Penguin Random House group of companies
whose addresses can be found at global.penguinrandomhouse.com

Penguin
Random House
UK

First published in Great Britain by Rider in 2020
Published in the United States by Harmony Books, an imprint of the Crown
Publishing Group, a division of Random House LLC, a Penguin Random House
Company, New York. www.crownpublishing.com
www.penguin.co.uk

A CIP catalogue record for this book is available from the British Library

Trade paperback ISBN 9781846046162
Hardback ISBN 9781846046841

Printed and bound in Great Britain by Clays Ltd, Elcograf S.p.A.

To all those who are creating
an awakened world

CONTENTS

MAKING YOUR PRACTICE RICHER

A Call to Wake Up

Dear Reader,

There are many good reasons to meditate, reasons that date back thousands of years. But this book was written not with a glance backward, but with a view forward. I call this the awakened life. It is synonymous with being in the light, finding grace, and being liberated from pain and suffering. It is the embodiment of true happiness. Total meditation is the key that unlocks them all.

If I can convince you that this is the life for you, what awaits is literally unimaginable. The things that are going to happen to you today, tomorrow, and for the rest of your life will no longer fall into predictable patterns. Every day will bring the experience of newness and creativity—if you allow happiness to unfold.

First, however, we have to ask the most basic question: What makes a person truly happy? A loving relationship, a settled family life, a successful career? There are probably as many answers as there are people in the world. But despite all our old ways of finding happiness, the ground under our feet is shifting. Something new, urgent, and exciting is happening. You will only become part of the change, however, by looking beneath the surface of your everyday life.

Everyone structures their happiness within a lifestyle. From day to day we make individual choices about things we'd like to do. For instance, do you want Chinese takeout for dinner? Maybe, maybe not. Have you checked your e-mail? Not yet, but you will. Surrounding these small daily choices is something bigger: the major decisions we've made about our individual lifestyle. Only in the last few decades has society begun to pay attention to the fact that your well-being depends crucially on your lifestyle.

You have the freedom to choose a poor lifestyle that includes tobacco, alcohol, no exercise, and a diet heavy in processed food. But do you really want to live like that? There's enough information available to avoid those heedless choices. As a result, better choices can be made, choices that involve pure foods, moving your body in beneficial ways, and honoring the environment. You might even ask, What is the absolute best lifestyle? This can be a life-changing question, and, if taken seriously, it transforms the very notion of what it means to be happy.

More and more people have made good lifestyle choices about diet, exercise, not smoking, and so on. But the key to the *best* lifestyle hasn't been found. Don't blame yourself. Modern secular society has some dominant trends that work against true, lasting well-being. Anxiety nibbles around the edge of almost everyone's life. The trends causing ever increasing loads of stress include:

- A faster and faster pace of living
- A deluge of distractions, including the Internet and video games
- Increasing rates of aging and dementia
- Rampant consumerism, spreading to more and more countries
- Dislocation and crumbling of traditional families
- An epidemic of anxiety and depression
- Global problems such as climate change, terrorism, pandemics, and refugeeism
- Collapse of trust in public institutions and politics
- Runaway disparity between rich and poor, along with racial disparity and injustice

These challenges are persistent and growing. You hear about them or experience them firsthand every day. Such massive challenges are inescapable, and individuals, as kindhearted as they may be, are powerless to solve them. Any single issue on the list is enough to overwhelm you if you get too close to it. Dealing with malaria in Africa, opiate addiction in the rust belt, suicide among veterans, or the looming prospect of Alzheimer's disease for the baby boomer generation—take any one of these problems and you can devote every waking hour attempting to solve it. Some people already are doing so, and while great strides are being made, the majority of our age-old problems still continue to exist.

For the average person, however, these threats provide a background of troubling chaos. You cannot put your head deep enough in the sand to be unaffected. The most enlightened diet, exercise, meditation, and yoga program do not provide a solution.

With that in mind, I set out to find the best lifestyle that ensures well-being despite the chaotic condition of the modern world. The best lifestyle can be described in a single phrase: *waking up*. Or, in other words, to be aware of everything around you. To wake up means devoting yourself to going beyond the everyday routines that people live by, the secondhand beliefs and opinions we have all adopted, the expectations we cling to, and the agenda of the ego. Waking up is about higher consciousness, or, in other words, a deeper awareness. Waking up is not a faraway goal—it can be your daily reality, starting here and now.

People still don't realize how all-important awareness is. To be aware is to notice something you didn't notice before: You become aware that the room is getting too warm, so you turn down the thermostat. You become aware that a friend hasn't called as often as they used to, so you call them to see how they are. These simple examples illustrate an important point. Nothing can be changed in your life unless you first become aware of it. This fact seems obvious as soon as it is stated, and yet there are depth, power, and possibilities in awareness that people rarely understand. What you can do with awareness will literally change every part of your life.

We validate reality with our mind. If your mind is truly open and free of confusion and conflict, reality will be perceived as a field of unlimited possibilities. If that sounds exaggerated, it's not—we have just learned to live with radically lowered expectations. We are trapped at a level of consciousness that fuels chaos and confusion, no matter how nicely we think our own life is going. Through a gradual development of bad physical, mental, psychological, and spiritual habits over the years, we have walled ourselves in. Being mind-made, the walls we have created are invisible but strong, sometimes impregnable.

As an illustration, let's imagine that a stranger, a clear-eyed, clairvoyant observer of human nature, followed you around today. There is no threat to you except that this stranger can read your mind. Here is what his notes might look like:

7:30 A.M.: Subject woke up, got out of bed, starting thinking and planning. Mental activity 90%, the same as yesterday.

8:30 A.M.: Conversation at breakfast table—typical exchanges. Subject leaves home for work, mental activity in neutral.

9:00 A.M.: Subject arrives at work. Mental activity falls into familiar grooves. Subject hopes today will be more exciting than yesterday.

11 A.M.: Subject immersed in work, starting to feel some stress from coworkers, boss, general environment.

NOON: Subject moves gratefully off to lunch. Mental activity relaxes as subject anticipates a pleasurable hour.

2:00 P.M.: Pleasant sensations from lunch have dissipated. Subject knuckles down to work again. Mental activity 80% of any day at work.

And so it continues. If asked for details, our clairvoyant observer would describe how often you repeat the same words and thoughts, exchange the same opinions, avoid the same unpleasantness, and so on, according to a set of fixed patterns that you do not deviate from very much. It would take a clairvoyant observer to discern these fixed patterns, because by and large we don't notice them. The unfortunate news is that a considerable portion of our day is spent being a robot of routine, repetition, and habit.

Do you really want to live like that?

WHAT YOU NEED TO DO

The process of waking up, of paying attention to our patterns and doing something different in life, needs to become continuous. It needs to become a lifestyle, because there is so much unconscious behavior in everyone's existence, even when seemingly everything is going our way.

It has perplexed me over the years that people are not really interested in their state of awareness, but I've come to know why. Whether we know it or not, each of us is fascinated by the mind's activity, meaning the constant stream of desires, fears, wishes, hopes, dreams, plans, expectations, and, for the fortunate, insights, intuition, and creative ideas. In other words, we become seduced by our thoughts. This can be alluring, distracting, and sometimes dangerous. By comparison, awareness is silent and still. It doesn't involve the same type of thinking that most of us use every day. You cannot watch it in motion or grab on to the next thing it does. Being uniform and constant, consciousness is taken for granted by everyone. As a result, we pay little attention to awareness, which in turn leads to a vicious circle: the less aware we are, the less we enact our power to shape our personal reality.

In the past, people needed so much help just to survive that they used awareness like a life jacket in a stormy sea. Pain and suffering were the norm; getting enough food was a daily struggle; the chance of falling prey to disease, accident, and violence was extremely high. In this context we see the rise of spiritual traditions that flourished in the earliest Vedic civilization in India, followed by Buddhism, Judaism, Christianity, and Islam. The naked fact is that everyday life was so filled with threats on every side that priests, gurus, saints, sages, and avatars had a ready-made and eager audience of people looking to transcend their dangerous existence.

Today, seeking an escape from the world has drastically diminished as a motivation for awareness, but the desire for transcendence is still within us. The most basic spiritual practices have become optional, and we choose our personal practice from a lavish menu the way we choose an entrée from a restaurant menu. People often pray or meditate to *escape* worldly cares and find something "higher." But I was struck by a comment from the noted Vietnamese Buddhist monk Thích Nhất Hạnh: "Meditation is not an evasion; it is a serene encounter with reality." This is what modern people need to hear. They need an incentive that makes meditation more than a choice on a menu.

Getting anyone to adopt the awakened life depends upon shifting gears in ways many might find drastic, as Thích Nhất Hạnh well understands:

> We do so much, we run so quickly, the situation is difficult, and many people say, "Don't just sit there, do something." But doing more things may make the situation worse. So you should say, "Don't just do something, sit there." Sit there, stop, be yourself first, and begin from there.

There's a beautiful simplicity in those words that has inspired me to write as simply as possible in this book, speaking informally as one person to another. I ask you, the reader, to take the same attitude, as if these pages were meant for you personally, because they are. In this book I want to highlight that there is such a thing as the best lifestyle. It is the awakened lifestyle. Nothing that's good in your present life has to be sacrificed—waking up expands every aspect of the good life. What's really at stake is making the decision to wake up, here and now. That's the first step in the direction of a future that really works, instead of a present that threatens to defeat us. What applies to meditation also applies to transformation: *Sit there, stop, be yourself first.*

Love,
Deepak

TOTAL MEDITATION:
A New and Better Way

1

Why "Total" Meditation?

If someone asked me what to expect from meditation, I'd reply, "Anything and everything." Meditation involves transformation. It affects every aspect of your well-being and can bring about positive change in your body, affect your mental outlook, increase your decision-making ability, and eliminate worry and anxiety. Meditation techniques are numerous—they can take you in a hundred different directions—but at heart they aim to answer one not so obvious question: Can existence take care of itself? If the answer is no, then all the struggle and frustration that enters everyday life is justified. You believe that nothing and no one are going to take care of you except yourself. That is why you are under so much stress.

However, if the answer is yes, a new life awaits everyone. The idea that existing—just being here right now—can bring fulfillment sounds objectionable, almost alien. It's not outlandish to your body, however. By their very nature, the cells in your body operate effortlessly. Likewise, your tissues and organs are effortlessly self-sustaining. In an average lifetime the heart beats a billion times, a prospect that baffles the mind, especially if you think of the heart as a machine that must keep pumping blood seamlessly without a glitch. No computer can be turned on a billion times and no airplane take off a billion times without the risk, or even certainty, of mechanical failure. But in the web of life, the heart—if, of course, it is healthy—undertakes its labors with complete lack of struggle. On average, our heart beats between 60 to 100 times a minute. Fascinating when you truly think about it. But then consider a shrew's heart, which beats 1,000 times a minute, or a hummingbird's, which can reach 1,250 beats per minute. The wonder is, their hearts work effortlessly, too.

The heart, while extraordinary, is by no means exceptional. In a normal healthy person, the community of organs—skin, heart, lungs, liver, brain—remains in balance and harmony quite effortlessly. But as we go about our daily activities, we rarely experience effortless harmony, either inside ourself or between ourself and others. Wars and domestic abuse have the same source in disharmony. Our worries are a symptom of disharmony, and if depression arises, it can sap the will to carry on. The notion that existence is enough seems ludicrous. But we can experience moments of equanimity, or even an extended period of equanimity, that at their fullest bring body, mind, and spirit into harmony. These interludes suggest that something more lasting can be achieved. That's why meditation is a journey and not just a calm break from one's daily routine.

If we can live knowing that existence can actually take care of itself at the level of the individual person, a radically new element will be added to modern life. We can live in a world in which there are no inner enemies like fear and anger roaming the mind beyond our control. Painful memories and unacceptable feelings will no longer be shoved down into the secret hiding places in the unconscious. We will be stirred from a state of virtual sleep that befalls us as mental dullness and inertia. (If you don't think we live in a state of virtual sleep, just look around at the expressionless faces of people glued to their smartphones or waiting at the airport.) The awakened life is energetic and fully conscious, erasing the woes that so often arise through our unconscious ways.

MEDITATION IS ABSOLUTELY UNIQUE

Personal transformation is what meditation provides once you embark on the journey. The first step is realizing that awareness in some form is always present. Thinking (in essence, judging) isn't the mind's true character. Awareness is. In the background of everything you do, the heart beats ceaselessly. In the background of everything you think, awareness watches ceaselessly as well. We take both for granted, but that doesn't remove their mystery and power. A research career can be spent in cardiology just to get a few steps closer to the hidden intricacies packed in a single heart cell. (It was recently discovered, to everyone's bafflement, that the heart has twelve taste receptors of the kind usually found in the mouth, and these receptors are most strongly attuned to bitter taste. No reasonable explanation exists, but then, we don't even know how the heart and circulatory system manage to maintain the same blood pressure in our toes and our head, despite the force of gravity.)

Recorded history has spent millennia trying to unravel the secrets of the human mind. Still, there is no consensus about how to explain consciousness and the ability to be aware of ourselves and the world around us. There is no alternative but to delve into your own awareness, which is where meditation begins. Meditation is practically the only human endeavor that explores the mind when it has no thoughts. Everything else in philosophy and psychology—or any other field of study—is about thoughts. Awareness precedes thoughts, but in modern life we have reversed things so completely that everyone's life is built upon mental activity without having the faintest idea where thoughts come from. Certainly, the brain is involved, but it hardly holds the key. Though we have made great strides in trying to understand the three-pound gray mass in our skulls, nothing about a brain cell indicates that it is processing thoughts, feelings, and sensations. There are some amazing medical cases in which a person's cerebral cortex, the thin layer on the outside of the brain responsible for higher thought, has been radically compressed by fluid pressure (so-called water on the brain, or hydrocephalus) beginning in infancy, and yet the person grew up without any sign, either to themselves or to others, that mental activity was impaired. Even more rarely, a benign growth can take over half of the cranial space or more, and yet once again the person seems mentally unaffected.

We think we get along well enough not knowing where thoughts come from, but that's not really so. In a fascinating TED talk in April 2019, a British theoretical physicist, David Deutsch, pointed out that throughout history the universe has been characterized as a war zone. In ancient societies, this war was envisioned as a war between good and evil, which became internalized in humans as good and bad impulses struggling inside us. In modern times, science has abandoned the old mythology but kept the war, making it a war between order and chaos. If this analogy sounds abstract, we can see it humanized in the current climate-change crisis as the struggle between a sustainable planet and a wasteland.

These are all mental models, however, and they have persisted for so long, Deutsch says, that we are victims of "cosmic monotony." Science has unwittingly continued the Old Testament notion that there is nothing new under the sun. What is the solution? Deutsch proposes that human beings are uniquely able to bring novelty into existence, which we do through new and deeper understanding. Thus as we wake up, the cosmos wakes up. In fact, Deutsch believes, the waking up has already begun, after billions of years of monotony.

The notion that human beings can make the universe wake up is very bold, but here is a physicist, someone who primarily deals with mathematical equations, putting consciousness front and center in the creative process. This extends a famous idea offered in the 1950s by the noted American physicist John Archibald Wheeler, who was the first to say that we live in a "participatory universe." In other words, everything we think is real "out there" depends on our beliefs, perceptions, observations, interpretations, and expectations "in here."

Leaving aside the cosmic implications, humans certainly create personal reality one individual at a time. What you make from the raw "stuff" of consciousness is unique to you. Therefore it makes perfect sense to explore how consciousness operates. There are rules and principles to be discovered, and what they determine is crucial to the way we all live our life.

THE PRINCIPLES OF CONSCIOUSNESS

Consciousness is awake and aware.

Consciousness crosses the boundaries of mind and body, matter and mind.

Consciousness is creative.

Once it creates something, consciousness keeps it in balance.

Consciousness is dynamic—it calls upon energy for action and change.

Consciousness is whole—it permeates everything in existence equally.

Consciousness is self-organizing—it oversees orderly systems and structures.

Consciousness is harmonious—every level of Nature is part of the whole. Every thread contributes to the cosmic tapestry.

These principles sound abstract, but they invisibly govern everything you think, say, and do. You speak intelligible thoughts, unlike the "word salad" of a schizophrenic, because your speech is orderly, organized, and regulated. A single memory, like the recollection of your sixth-birthday party, must be retrieved from scattered areas of the brain, where every memory is stored in fragments. Only by a nearly instantaneous reassembly do you have a coherent memory. When you remember something, a mental jigsaw puzzle is put together in consciousness. Likewise, you recognize faces thanks to several coordinated brain regions. At an even more basic level, you see a world of color through a complex process that knowingly fashions over two million shades of recognizable color from red, blue, and green, the only three wavelengths of light your retina responds to.

All this occurs without the processes knowing anything about the principles of consciousness. The proteins that construct your body number more than 100,000, perhaps up to a million, yet each is distinct. Each does its singular job precisely while whizzing past thousands of other proteins like random dust particles, and each acquired knowledge of what to do in some mysterious way unfathomable by the human mind.

Why is all of this important to meditation? Enormous benefits will arise from your understanding firsthand how consciousness operates. This understanding is what makes waking up unique. Waking up isn't the same as thinking, nor is it the same as being sharp instead of groggy, smart instead of dull. Waking up is about learning how consciousness operates and then applying its principles accordingly. No other knowledge is like this, and none is more valuable.

What became known as the world's religions, spiritual traditions, and wisdom schools have grown into a mountain of texts and teachings. Yet awareness demands little. To be aware is a simple state. A one-day-old baby looks around without comprehension, but it is aware nonetheless. Not yet understanding anything about its life, a newborn baby is prepared to understand everything that will unfold. Many babies have an irresistible smile on their faces. They know joy without knowing what joy is.

Most important, being aware aligns you with the creative impulse in Nature. If meditation is all about awareness, what we can accomplish is virtually unlimited.

TOTAL MEDITATION

The kind of meditation I am advocating in this book is called *total meditation* because it embraces all the principles of consciousness that exist to be understood and lived. The other kinds of meditation that are typically taught, no matter what school or tradition they belong to, are different. They are occasional meditations, practiced at a certain time of day, using a specific technique before going about the rest of the day as usual. Such an approach is like practicing the piano or your tennis swing—the hope is that the more you practice, the better you will get at it. While occasional meditation has its benefits—for instance, it can calm you down and lower your pulse rate temporarily—it is seriously limited. The few minutes a day spent in meditation are powerless to overcome the overwhelming flood of experiences outside meditation.

The briefness of occasional meditation doesn't undermine the process—a huge amount of research validates the practice. Meditation cannot be blamed for losing the battle to change modern life when it was designed, centuries ago, against the relative stasis of lives spent on farms, in temples, and around family life. Even then, however, it was realized that total immersion in meditation was the ultimate answer to pain and suffering as well as the path to freedom. Traditional Indian life was divided into four stages, or *ashramas*, and the last, which was undertaken in late middle age, was a kind of double retirement. The person retired from work and family obligations, went into seclusion, and retired within themselves through meditation.

Total immersion was also a choice for the few who were natural renunciates, who longed for an inward existence in place of work and family life. But neither model suits modern life or our newfound taste and widespread quest for personal spirituality. In this book, I want to go even further by offering a kind of total immersion that isn't traditional or even "spiritual" in a religious sense (and where you don't have to give up your day job). As I've just outlined, total meditation is an exploration of how consciousness works, with the goal of applying those principles to your own life.

For the vast majority of people who try occasional meditation, know that your practice gives you a taste of total meditation, a taste of stillness. This taste can be revealing, no doubt, because most people have had no extended experience of "quiet mind." If they know what inner peace feels like, they still cannot call upon it whenever they want. However pleasant as it is to find peace and inner quiet in meditation, once you open your eyes, what does the mind do? It returns to the life it knows, a constant stream of worries, desires, demands, duties, wishes, hopes, and fears. Still, occasional meditation, while limited, can take the edge off, so to speak, and can often be the first step toward transformation in your life.

My taking up meditation in the early 1980s was a turning point in my life. Looking back, I see a stressed Boston doctor in his thirties who left the house before dawn and returned after sunset, and whose jangled nervous system seemed to need a daily supply of cigarettes and alcohol to settle itself down. I fell into those habits because every doctor around me back then, especially the overworked interns and residents, followed the same *lifestyle.*

Within a year of my starting to take time out twice a day to practice a simple mantra meditation, my bad habits had fallen away completely. I knew firsthand the powerful change that could happen to anyone. Within a few years, it became my mission to teach meditation to as many people as I could. I have kept on teaching ever since and have taught various techniques. Countless people have learned to meditate from me, and even if I met each person only briefly, I was certain in my heart that meditation would change their life.

Unfortunately, I came to see that there was a wide gap between the potential of what meditation could do and what it actually does. Part of the reason for this disconnect is that people give meditation only half a chance. They try it for a while, only to begin to skip their daily meditation because their days are too busy, and very soon they drop their practice, sometimes with the excuse that "I tried to meditate, but it didn't work." Or they seek a specific benefit like lowering their blood pressure, but getting results took too much patience compared with taking a pill. There are other factors, too: the disapproval of family and friends (far more likely thirty years ago than now, but the possibility still exists) or a fear of seeming strange and becoming isolated socially as someone who wanders off to the next bright, shiny object in the spiritual marketplace.

THE DIVIDED SELF

Eventually I saw that the problem lay much deeper, not in modern lifestyles but in the divided self that leads to such lifestyles. The divided self is something we all live with. Every day we put on different hats, depending on who we are relating to. We are different at home than at work, different with family than with strangers, different in our private thoughts than in the words we speak.

Meditation is like having all the king's horses and all the king's men trying to put Humpty-Dumpty together again.

People can feel different forces contending inside themselves. A simple decision like choosing to lose five pounds becomes a struggle between the voices in our head, representing what we want to do on one side and why we cannot get there on the other (habit, inertia, impulsive desires, compulsive behavior, giving in to temptation, and so on). Ultimately, the forces of division win and the diet fails. You can't put Humpty-Dumpty together again when *you* are Humpty-Dumpty. No one from the outside can repair another person's divided self, and since the divided self is embedded so deep, it cannot repair itself, either.

Most people don't know the terms *divided self* or *fragmented self*, but look at one of its by-products everyone does know about—our collective fascination with fame. We are stoked by mass media to believe that movie stars and other celebrities are lovely, special creatures. Not only do they look beautiful, each has a perfect love life and the most fulfilling kind of lifestyle. The reality is quite different, of course, and the other side of the coin is our relish at reading about a celebrity's downfall through drugs, a failed relationship, or some kind of scandal. It's an old story that people crave idols to worship, only to tear them down.

What we're indulging in through celebrity worship is wish fulfillment. Forced to live with our own divided selves, we project perfection, which is wholeness, onto celebrities. We fantasize that they are privileged creatures who are exempt from reality. In our own life there are constant ups and downs, stretches of boredom, endless routine, and the grip of bad habits we cannot kick. We need to see that these limitations are the products of the divided self. Wish fulfillment doesn't really help you when it comes to facing your own life. The journey of total meditation can.

The divided and fragmented self cannot do its own healing. It will continue to face ups and downs, inner contradictions, confusion, and conflict. If you look at yourself honestly, the flaws you see today have probably existed for years. If you are anxious and depressed today, it is highly unlikely to be the first time. If you give in to a bad habit like overeating, that habit has a history of actions and decisions. If you have negative psychological tendencies—such as a short temper, or giving in too easily to other people, or thinking of yourself as a victim—those traits also have a history. The momentum of life continues to roll along because when you try to fight against an ingrained habit, the struggle is between two aspects of the divided self. The aspect that wants to change faces off against the aspect that stubbornly refuses to change. The typical result is that neither wins, and the face-off continues.

The excitement that I first felt about meditation—and which countless people have also felt when they began to meditate— came from the discovery that there is a place inside everyone that is free of the divided self. Quiet and inner peace are good experiences, but their real importance lies in escaping inner conflict, turmoil, fear, depression, worry, confusion, and self-doubt. With a little practice, anyone can find this place inside, go there, and have the experience of a self that is whole and untroubled. Making that experience last is another matter.

WAKING UP, HERE AND NOW

The issue isn't whether meditation can take you beyond the divided self—it can, without a doubt. The issue is how to heal the divided self, because the moment you open your eyes at the end of a meditation, the divided self returns to business as usual. As things stand, the only solution to this problem is based on repetition. If you just keep meditating day after day, year after year, everything will be resolved. "Stick with it" is good advice, and the promise that is held out—that one day you will be whole—is valid in rare cases. The tradition of meditation is thousands of years old in the East, and there are countless records of people waking up, becoming enlightened, finding wholeness, reaching unity consciousness—call it whatever you like.

Waking up is a real phenomenon, and it often occurs quite unpredictably. In *Walden*, Thoreau writes of "the solitary hired man on a farm in the outskirts of Concord, who has had his second birth." (The very phrase *second birth* goes back to Vedic India many centuries ago.) Thoreau's stay at Walden Pond was a symbol for the inner journey of waking up, which is the goal and natural outcome of meditation. He expressed how timeless and vast the experience feels when he wrote, "Zoroaster, thousands of years ago, travelled the same road and had the same experience, but he, being wise, knew it to be universal."

Winter at Walden Pond was brutally cold, and Thoreau experienced conditions scarcely less harsh that the proverbial yogi sitting in the high altitude of a Himalayan cave. That image of hardship and privation has reinforced the notion, now stubbornly embedded in all cultures, that devoting oneself to meditation is arduous. Along with physical hardship, some other requirements sound very unpleasant. They range from worldly renunciation to mortification of the flesh, isolation from society, and, at the most extreme demand, a willingness in the name of God to be martyred (the sacrifice to be followed by waking up in Heaven to a blessed reward).

The overall effect of these embedded notions has been to discourage the average person from considering that higher consciousness might be within reach for anyone in daily life. However, waking up is rare only because we label it that way. Society sets apart those who have become enlightened, saintly, or spiritually advanced, however you want to put it. Marginality isn't the same as rejection, though. In an age of faith, such figures were set apart to be revered. Today, when faith in a higher power has grown more suspect, these individuals are more likely to be viewed as outsiders from normal life, to be admired, shrugged off, or forgotten.

With this in mind, I searched for a way to make waking up part of normal life. First and foremost, *total meditation had to be natural and effortless*, because without that, meditation will keep falling short. A path that demands months and years of repetition using a fixed technique is far from being natural or effortless. Many people who begin the practice wonder if they are meditating correctly. Many others find the whole enterprise foreign to how they live—the average busy household doesn't have much in common with a temple, monastery, or ashram. But the process that takes us closer to quiet mind and inner peace may be simpler than most of us think. We get glimpses of quiet mind in the presence of great art and music. We experience inner peace (hopefully) every night as we fall asleep after a day that has been enjoyable and untroubled (if we don't experience this, every young child does). These glimpses come naturally and effortlessly.

Besides being effortless and natural, *total meditation must be spontaneous*. It must happen in the present moment as spontaneously as an unexpected burst of happiness or being struck by the beauty of a gorgeous sunset. In that way, waking up can flow in the here and now, merging into whatever else you are doing.

Finally, *total meditation must be in line with each person's own ultimate desires*. It's only natural to want more out of life, yet unfortunately the spiritual framework that surrounds meditation in many instances condemns desire. For thousands of years, desires, particularly of the flesh, were said to lower humans to the level of animals. Worldly desires supposedly pull us too much into the endless pursuit of external things like money and success. Succumbing to our passions supposedly undermines morality. What might bring short-term enjoyment supposedly won't bring lasting happiness. These are familiar arguments, yet desire in itself is not a bad thing.

We cannot escape desire and shouldn't be told that we must. Life unfolds through desire in every form, and winnowing out the higher desires, such as desiring to reach God, doesn't succeed in practice. The so-called lower desires are inevitably part of the human experience. To reject them just reinforces the divided self.

If these three requirements are met—if waking up is natural and effortless, spontaneous, and in line with our personal desires—then the divided self can come to an end. It will take this entire book to support such a claim, because looking around, none of us sees someone who is whole and undivided. We cannot be blamed for assuming that there is no escape. Human nature simply is what it has always been. But waking up has always existed as well, and when it happens, consciousness does the healing that the divided self cannot accomplish on its own.

TOTAL MEDITATION

Lesson 1: Being Aware

In this book you will learn to expand your awareness, to make it deeper, and, ultimately, to wake up to a new reality. To do all this you must firmly understand what awareness is. To begin with, awareness is an experience, the most basic experience possible. If you become aware of rain suddenly beginning to fall, awareness experiences change. If you are sitting calmly with your eyes closed and feel peaceful, awareness experiences the stillness of nonchange. Life may change, and sometimes it doesn't, but awareness notices it all.

Here are a few ways to make you aware of awareness:

- Put down this book and listen to any sound that occurs around you. By hearing the sound, you know you are present here and now. When you see, touch, taste, or smell anything, you also know that you exist here and now. Knowing that you are present is awareness.

  Now turn your attention away from the sound and ignore it. You are still present even when you ignore the five senses. Awareness is more basic than sights, sounds, tastes, textures, or smells. Our senses fill the mind with content, but awareness needs no content. Simply being here is the ground state of awareness.

- Look at this book, then close your eyes and see it in your mind's eye. Think the word *book*, then say the word aloud. What do these four experiences have in common? They were experienced in awareness. Words, thoughts, and images constantly change, but the recording medium doesn't change—this is awareness.
- Sit still for a moment and make your mind a blank. After a bit, the blankness will turn into a thought, image, or sensation. When this happens, make your mind a blank again. Watch as the blankness is replaced by a new thought, image, or sensation. Yet no matter whether your mind is empty or has something in it, you are always there. You have a sense of self that exists no matter what is happening or not happening. That sense of self is awareness.

TOTAL CONSCIOUSNESS AND YOU

Now that I've outlined the goal and structure of total meditation, let's go deeper into the question that opened this chapter, a question that underlies everything: Can existence take care of itself? The answer is yes, Consciousness upholds creation. At this moment, and every moment since you were born, you are surrounded by the infinite intelligence and creative power of consciousness. I know these principles can be a little difficult to grasp in the beginning, but stay with me, because they are important for entering into total meditation.

If Nature holds one secret that makes life on Earth understandable, it is this: Life *is* consciousness. You already know that you *have* consciousness. Without it you would be mindless. The principles that consciousness follows permeate everything. It is mistaken to believe, as many scientists automatically assume, that consciousness didn't appear until the human brain evolved. The most basic life forms follow the principles of consciousness by being self-organized and knowing exactly how to stay alive. These principles hold true even among life forms we consider totally primitive.

In 1973 a woman in Texas noticed a peculiar yellow blob that had sprung up in her backyard the way "fairy rings," sudden growths of toadstools, can appear overnight. But the blob wasn't a toadstool or anything the woman could recognize.

Biologists were consulted, and although the yellow blob quickly died, it was identified as a kind of slime mold, a life form going back at least a billion years. There was a flurry of publicity around this new variety, named *Physarum polycephalum*, but then it was forgotten until October 2019, when the Paris Zoological Park announced that it was putting the yellow blob on exhibit as a most extraordinary phenomenon. As CNN reported it, the blob

is bright yellow, can creep along at a speed of up to 4 centimeters (1.6 inches) per hour, can solve

> problems even though it doesn't have a brain and
> can heal itself if it is cut in two. . . . [It] is neither
> a plant, an animal, nor a fungus. It doesn't have
> two sexes, male and female—it has 720. And it can
> also split into different organisms and then fuse
> back together

As a strange biological curiosity, *Physarum polycephalum* created a sensation, but there is a deep mystery to consider here. Slime molds are incredibly basic life forms. There are nine hundred species, formerly classified as fungi but now given their own loosely organized kingdom. There is no real connection between the species except that they can function either as single-celled organisms or clumped together in a large community. In one part of their life cycle, they have the appearance of gelatinous slime.

The mystery is how a life form barely more complex than green algae floating as pond scum could be intelligent. When a study in the prestigious *Proceedings of the Royal Society* announced that the yellow blob could solve problems, the researchers meant that it could avoid noxious substances and remember what they were for up to a year. The blob also seemed able to find the quickest route to escape a labyrinth. Never mind that slime mold, which thrives on damp forest floors, is almost immortal. When faced with its only foes, light and drought, it can hibernate for several years and spring back to life again.

This is certainly an example of how existence takes care of itself, which is displayed by how the yellow blob exhibits qualities of consciousness. Besides being self-organizing and self-sustaining, it adapts to its surroundings, knows how to avoid toxins that threaten it, and solves problems.

There is no mystery to this if you accept that consciousness is part of existence. The two go together because they must, according to everything we observe about life. If existence was a blank, a tabula rasa, there is no physical force with the ability to create consciousness. Blankness is dead. Consciousness is alive. You can't turn deadness into life, and yet obviously life appeared. So the obvious conclusion is that life was generated in the field of consciousness, which is alive already but invisible until consciousness takes physical form.

Here we do not need to be concerned with the metaphysical side of the argument. Our project is more practical: testing to see if a hypothesis is true—in this case, the hypothesis that existence can take care of us effortlessly, naturally, and spontaneously. Total meditation aims to prove that despite the divided self and all the problems it has created, consciousness has not abandoned human beings. It gives us the capacity to take care of our own life effortlessly by doing what every life form down to the yellow blob is doing: relying on the principles of consciousness. The only difference is that we have the choice whether to align with these principles or not. This choice escapes most people, however. The divided self has done its worst by disconnecting us from our source and then convincing us that this disconnect is normal.

THE WAY BACK

Any viable meditation will give you the experience of silent awareness, but the experience is often temporary and not very deep. You can close your eyes, sit still, and arrive at a similar experience (assuming that you aren't agitated or stressed beforehand). What makes meditation different from simply closing your eyes is its ability to take you deeper into silent awareness. In Sanskrit this experience is known as *samadhi*. Yogis who can sit in samadhi deeply enough are able to do extraordinary things like slowing down their heart rate and reducing their oxygen consumption to a bare minimum. They can even raise their internal body temperature to the point that they can sit in the freezing cold without harm while wearing only a thin silk robe or nothing at all.

As a personal experience, samadhi shows us the difference between shallow silence and deep silence. In shallow silence, however, some important things can still happen. It was only recently discovered, for example, that simply by closing your eyes and engaging in slow, regular breathing, you can overcome stress. This technique, known as *vagal breathing*, represents a real breakthrough because of its simplicity and effectiveness. I've covered vagal breathing in previous books, but it is worth repeating here.

Vagal breathing takes its name from the vagus nerve, the longest and most complex of the ten cranial nerves that connect the brain with the rest of the body. The Latin word *vagus* means "wanderer," and the vagus nerve certainly wanders. It links the brain with the heart, lungs, and abdomen, all areas that are highly sensitive to stress. The vagus nerve is also an afferent, or sensory, nerve, meaning that it transmits bodily sensations to the brain, including reactions associated with stress. The brain then sends signals in response, setting up a constant feedback loop. When you find yourself in a stressful situation, your heart rate goes up; you breathe in shallow, irregular bursts; and you feel tightness in your stomach and gut.

This circuitry of stress has been mapped and understood for a long time, but it also needed to be understood in reverse, meaning the circuitry of stress reduction. Searching for how meditation actually works in physical terms, researchers followed the clues left by breathing. So-called yogic breathing, for example, consists of exercises that control the breath, making it more regular, slower, and deeper. It turns out that regular, relaxed breathing is regulated by the vagus nerve, with its direct connection to brain, heart, and lungs. By stimulating the vagus nerve, you can induce the relaxation response. This discovery led to the widely publicized practice of vagal breathing, which is a quite simple way to stimulate the vagus nerve.

VAGAL BREATHING

An effective remedy in stressful situations

Step 1: Sit quietly with eyes closed.

Step 2: Easily breathe in to the count of four.

Step 3: Breathe out to the count of four, then pause for a count of one.

Step 4: Repeat for 5 minutes.

Given its total simplicity, vagal breathing helps not only to relieve stress but also to manage anger and anxiety. Medical research is also exploring the use of electrical vagus nerve stimulation in the treatment of various psychological and physical diseases. My coauthor Dr. Rudolph E. Tanzi of Harvard Medical School and I reported the possibilities in our book *The Healing Self:*

> What's mind bending, as viewed from conventional medical training, is how wide the possible benefits of vagus nerve stimulation (VNS) seem to be. Presently no less than thirty-two disorders are undergoing research, with indications of positive results. They begin with alcohol addiction, irregular heartbeat (atrial fibrillation), and autism, and run through a rogue's gallery of physical and psychological illnesses: heart disease, mood disorders like depression and anxiety, a variety of intestinal disorders, addictions, and perhaps even memory loss and Alzheimer's disease.

The possibilities of such research are unfolding rapidly, but what's important for us here is that medical research has shown that the meditative state is natural and effortless. The shallow silence that is experienced even with a brief exposure to meditation achieves relaxation through the vagus nerve, and there is no separation between the physical and the mental side of relaxation. If shallow silence is so easily accessible, the deeper silence of samadhi should be just as natural and accessible.

The "wandering" nerve is not simply carrying signals all over the body, it is conveying consciousness. The fact that a single cranial nerve has holistic effects indicates how totally consciousness pervades mind and body. There isn't just one mind-body connection. The totality of consciousness is at work, which is why total meditation will work. You aren't fixing one thing at a time. You reconnect to the totality of consciousness. In that way you prove to yourself, as meditation unfolds, that existence can take care of you.

Consciousness gives of itself without reservation. When the tiniest speck of life on Earth appeared almost four billion years ago, it was more primitive than a bacterium. It had no DNA. It wasn't even a one-celled creature like an amoeba. Yet just as a single fertilized egg in the womb has the entire structure of a human being in it, the first signs of primordial life were products of total, infinite consciousness. (Perhaps we should stop assigning a date to the origins of life. Nobel laureate in physics Brian Josephson has written, "Matter is alive and can make decisions," which sounds like the utterance of a mystic. In fact, the ability of atoms to behave outside the predictions of fixed laws has been a mystery for more than a century, ever since the advent of quantum physics.)

TOTAL MEDITATION

Lesson 2: Not "In Here," Not "Out There"

We think it is only natural to divide mental experiences "in here" from physical experiences "out there." For the sake of convenience, I use those terms here. But the sea of consciousness embraces everything, without boundaries and limitations. Because you *are* consciousness, you are free to respect boundaries—being awake doesn't mean you get to walk on the grass if the sign says not to—while at the same time knowing that the boundaries are artificial. They don't change your essential nature, which is unbounded.

To show how easily you can cross the line between "in here" and "out there," here's an exercise that erases the dividing line instantly:

- Take your fingers and run them across something that has a rough texture, such as sandpaper. Immediately close your eyes and feel the same rough texture mentally.
- Dip your hand in ice water, then immediately imagine the same freezing sensation.
- Gaze on a crimson rose, then close your eyes and see it again "in here."

There is no difference in where these experiences are located. They are not exclusively "out there" or "in here," but in consciousness, which embraces both. If you imagine at this moment the texture of sandpaper, the cold of ice water, or the sight of a rose, these sensations aren't as intense mentally as the physical sensation. But consider how vivid a dream can be. The things you see are as lifelike as in their physical appearance. The same goes for sounds heard in a dream. A small proportion of people can even go beyond sight and sound, being able to smell, taste, and touch in their dreams. Going that far isn't necessary, however. The reality produced in dreams is as real for you as any experience "out there," because dreams have the same basis in consciousness. (If you're not convinced, think back to a time when you were startled awake from a nightmare. If that wasn't a real experience, then why did you awake in a panic?)

Life always knows what to do, even if we doubt that we do. No one had to teach your heart how to beat. Humble skin cells undertake processes as complex as those in a brain cell. Red blood corpuscles, the only cells in your body that lack DNA, are regulated to know where to take their load of oxygen and when to unload it. Where does this knowing come from? In medical school, the brain is identified as the seat of consciousness, an assumption that has spread through society as common knowledge, but it is totally wrong, a mistaken notion born of pride.

Let's drop the whole mistaken belief that limits consciousness to the thinking mind and assign it instead to everything in Nature. Let me offer a remarkable example of how totally consciousness upholds life. You might consider this example a digression from the topic of meditation, but I find it too fascinating to resist.

I'm going to describe a miracle of Nature, one that begins with a small Australian seabird known as Gould's petrel (*Pterodroma leucoptera*). This bird is nondescript—about ten inches long, brown and gray above and white below—but its life cycle is so astonishing as to defy rational explanation.

Off the east coast of Australia lies Cabbage Tree Island, named for a kind of palm tree that covers it. When a fuzzy gray chick is born, a pair of Gould's petrels start feeding it by going out to sea and returning with filled crops that regurgitate fish into the chick's yawning mouth. This ritual occurs every night for three months. Then one night the parent birds fail to return. The chick waits. No parents show up, night after night. The chick begins to starve.

But instead of dying from hunger, the chick is motivated to escape its plight. Gould's petrels nest on the ground in rock crevices covered by fallen palm fronds. The chick peers out, then ventures to the bottom of a nearby cabbage tree. It has never flown before, but somehow the chick knows that flight is its only escape.

Like albatrosses and other seabirds that are ungainly on land, a Gould's petrel cannot take off unless it is helped by a breeze, and the forest floor of Cabbage Tree Island is dead still. The chick therefore decides to climb to the top of a tree to launch itself into the air. No one shows the baby bird the way, and it has never performed this feat. But up it goes, using curved claws and beak to ascend, stopping to rest when it must by wrapping its wings around the trunk. Weakened by hunger, the chick has only one chance to climb the tree. If it falls, it dies.

Once the fledgling makes its ascent, its perils aren't quite over, because the crown of a cabbage tree is outfitted with sharp, spiny thorns on which the chick can get caught. If it makes it through this trap, it throws itself out into the air, another life-or-death moment. The wind has to favor the bird, and it must use its wings to fly rather than simply drop back to earth, which would be fatal.

Should the chick successfully mount the breeze, the most remarkable part of the story commences. For the next five to six years a Gould's petrel never sees land again. Constantly soaring and feeding from the surface of the sea, they sleep, perhaps as little as forty minutes a night, by alternating which side of the brain is sleeping or awake . . . in midflight! Eventually they return from their travels all over the Tasman Sea to the same dot of an island where they were born—an island smaller by comparison than a single period on a sheet of typing paper. There they mate and their life cycle begins again.

Reflect upon the overlapping mysteries involved in this one subspecies of bird. Naturalists can observe Gould's petrel and describe its behavior, but every step defies explanation. To say that instinct or genetics guides the fledgling is the best that science can do at this time. But consider this: DNA has only one function, to produce the major proteins and enzymes that structure a cell. The blueprint of a cell isn't alive. How would DNA tell a petrel on its maiden flight to look down until it sees tiny squid and fish just below the surface of the water, and then to dive, skim the surface, and catch its prey, a complex maneuver at the best of times, which the petrel has never seen performed?

Instinct fares no better, because there has to be a basis for how each step is timed in the petrel's first flight, and the only signal involved is hunger, which drives the chick out of its hole in the rocks. Where did it get the specific behavior of climbing a palm tree, a feat for which it is very poorly equipped, even with sharp claws? Instinct is basically a way of fudging our ignorance, palming off complex behaviors throughout the animal kingdom as somehow built in. How remains a complete mystery.

Everything a petrel chick does exhibits conscious traits. It has an intention. It knows what it needs to do. It acts according to a time schedule, and it doesn't need teaching, possessing every bit of knowledge innately. Unless all these things are coordinated, any single step on the way to taking flight will not work. In fact, the whole chain of behaviors must exist to avoid fatal consequences at every step. Even the fact that a petrel chick gorges on food until it weighs a third more than its parents prepares it for the famine when the parents mysteriously fail to return one night. The petrel then must subsist on its body fat for two weeks.

What seems undeniable is that this bird doesn't know just one thing or another. It knows everything necessary for its existence.

The only viable explanation for the intricate behavior of Gould's petrel lies beyond instinct and genes, in consciousness alone. Consciousness expresses itself through intelligent, orderly, creative ways. The result is that existence can take care of itself and, by extension, us.

TOTAL MEDITATION
Lesson 3: Inner Knowing

The mind of a two-year-old child is active and curious, hungry to know everything that is happening around them. From this beginning we grow up to know all manner of things. These things get compiled into our personal fund of knowledge, whether this involves speaking French or learning to roller-skate. But knowledge isn't the same as knowingness, which comes first. There is a state of inner knowing that everyone has. It is innate. You cannot be conscious without it. In meditation we deepen our inner knowing, but first we need to recognize what knowing is.

Here are a few ways to make you aware of inner knowing.

- Say aloud the following sentence: *He went to the kitchen to pare a pair of pears.* Immediately you know by ear that these three words with the same sound mean three different things. You didn't have to sort them out separately. Instead, you possess silent inner knowingness that works instantly.

- A woman was waiting at the hospital emergency room for two hours without being seen. Running out of patience, she goes to the nurses' station and says, "I've been waiting for two hours. How many doctors work here anyway?" The nurse in charge looks up and says, "About half." Why is this funny? Because you know a joke when you hear one. There is no mental need to work it out. Humor strikes instantly, as does all inner knowing.

- Look around the room and notice the things in it—furniture, rugs on the floor, paintings on the wall, perhaps another person. You recognize what everything is, a basic quality of inner knowing. But now experience the room in a different way. Look again and notice only the colors of everything. How do you know that color even exists? This is a deeper inner knowing. It is built into human awareness to such a degree that you can differentiate up to two million different shades of color. Yet the existence of color by itself comes from an inner knowing that cannot be put into words—and doesn't need to be. You know color innately, not by reading about it or being taught by someone else.

Your retina is physically bombarded by photons, giving rise to the mechanics of sight. Coded chemical information begins to course through the optic nerves leading from the eye to the brain. These data have no color in them, however, because photons are colorless, and so are nerve signals. Color is known in consciousness alone. That's how the quality of knowingness is embedded in existence. You couldn't be here without knowingness, which applies not just to color but to all five senses.

The human condition—namely the complex and conflicting characteristics of who we are—has been lamented for centuries, but there is a counterview that offers a solution. It looks on total consciousness as a reality that permeates human life as completely as it permeates everything in Nature—but with a difference. We can take control of it. Total consciousness isn't a force outside us that acts like a master puppeteer dangling us on invisible strings. Thanks to free will, *Homo sapiens* long ago snapped the strings. We unfold our potential according to our own desires. We have aspirations, which no other living creature can claim to have.

No one threw us out of the natural order. We leaped out of our own accord. We make up our own mind, and, with the freedom to aspire, civilizations rise and fall. The ultimate aspiration survives the fall of empires, though. It is the aspiration to experience total consciousness and the transformation that comes with it. Is it possible to actually access the consciousness that governs the cosmos and the smallest speck of life? The answer is yes, but it will take a whole chapter to unpack what *yes* really means.

2

Your Life
Is Your Meditation

Meditation gives us access to higher consciousness. Higher consciousness can go by a number of names—pure consciousness, cosmic consciousness, or enlightenment. (All these names have a ring of falseness, which I will get to in a minute. Names take away magic, and there is so much magic in consciousness that we must never lose sight of it.)

Meditation has acquired a mystical reputation going back thousands of years, because the portal to higher consciousness is seemingly closed to the everyday mind. In this book, I am proposing a radical rethinking. Meditation isn't something otherworldly. It is quite natural. In fact, we have all been meditating since birth. Each of us has experienced, one time or another, every state reachable by the techniques taught by meditation teachers. This must be true, because if meditation didn't reflect what the mind is already doing, it couldn't be taught. It couldn't even exist. Higher mathematics isn't mystical, because everyone uses numbers. Exquisite cuisine isn't otherwordly, because (almost) everyone can boil an egg.

If you can grasp the essence of a thing, everything else is simply more complicated. The essence of math and cooking doesn't change just because they can be raised to the level of an art. The same is true of consciousness. You and I have spent a lifetime going in and out of meditation mode, as we will call it here. Generically, meditation mode is any mental state that looks inward, and over the centuries, these mental states have acquired names:

Mindfulness

Self-inquiry

Reflection

Contemplation

Concentration

Prayer

Quiet mind

Controlled breathing

Bliss

Just as higher mathematics or haute cuisine is an art, these practices belong to the art of meditation. But, in essence, meditation mode exists in everyone to serve a basic purpose that is totally necessary. Your mind goes into meditation mode out of the need to be in balance. All meditation practices stem from this need, so we must try to understand it. The deeper our understanding, the more valid total meditation will be.

STAYING IN BALANCE

Balance is one of those words that has become exhausted through overuse. Besides all the messages we receive about balanced exercise and diet, all kinds of products, from vitamins and breakfast cereals to hair products and shoes, use "balance" as a selling point. But to a physiologist, balance is necessary for life itself.

If you push your body out of balance by shoveling snow off the driveway or jogging around the park, as soon as you stop that activity, your heart rate and blood pressure, the oxygen use in your muscles, and your digestive and immune systems will automatically return to homeostasis, the state of balance when your body is at rest. Every bodily function knows how to return to home base. The capacity to regroup and rebalance is embedded in us.

In his entertaining and hugely informative 2019 book *The Body*, Bill Bryson unfolds just how mysterious homeostasis is. In fact, the book rests on the premise that despite advanced medical research, almost everything about the human body remains a mystery. No one knows why, for example, we hiccup or why we sleep. Or why we are the only mammals who do not produce our own vitamin C, or who have so many allergies, or who run the risk of choking to death while eating. Our uniqueness has some strange byways. Human beings inhabit all kinds of climates from the alpine to the tropical, but we exist within a slim margin of temperature internally. Increase your body temperature by two degrees Fahrenheit and you begin to be feverish. Lower it by one and a half degrees and you begin to feel chilly, and at 95°F hypothermia begins to set in.

Your body goes to extraordinary lengths to maintain equilibrium at a core temperature of approximately 98.6°F, as Bryson illustrates through a notable experiment in which a man ran a marathon on a treadmill under controlled conditions. The temperature in the room was lowered until it was very cold, far below freezing, then steadily raised until it was very hot, well above all but the hottest desert. but in either case the subject's body temperature didn't vary by more than a single degree Celsius. The fact that the two processes that cool and heat the body, namely sweating and shivering, seem so basic doesn't make our physical equilibrium any less astonishing.

Something similar happens in the mind, but invisibly. There is a resting place for mental equilibrium, too, and when we stray out of balance, our mind knows how to return home. We go into meditation mode. This fact has been substantiated in various ways that do not seem, at first glance, to be related to meditation. A prime example is emotions. Just as with the body, everyone has a set point for their mood, a level of contentment they return to after an emotional event is over, whether the event is happy or sad. One person's emotional set point can be very different from another person's, which is why we notice people who seem naturally happy or naturally glum. There is no scientific explanation for this disparity. The most disruptive events are no obstacle. Within six months, the memory of an event will remain, but not the disrupted mood.

Sad love songs exaggerate when they speak of being heartbroken forever. One of the most popular jukebox selections of all time is Patsy Cline's rendition of Willie Nelson's "Crazy," which begins, "Crazy, I'm crazy for feeling so lonely." But just wait six months and, for most people, the "craziness" will pass.

If emotions return to home base, what about the mind and all our random and sometimes wild thoughts? The notion that the mind rebalances itself is new. Sometimes we can become consumed with all the activity whirling around in our head. We rarely take a pause from thinking to notice that awareness is a constant background. This background isn't passive. It draws us back into equilibrium, just as homeostasis draws the body back. Because consciousness is a totality, it is artificial to draw a distinction between physical and mental balance—when you calm down after a heated argument, a sudden fright, or a bout of worry, your cells are also calming down from the imbalance your emotional state created for them.

This whole discussion underlines the point that meditation wouldn't work unless the mind already had a rebalancing mechanism. Meditation brings consciousness into view from its hiding place in the background. It's not as if meditation is a discovery by ancient Eastern mystics. It only deepens and extends what the mind naturally does already, the way that a long, warm massage deepens the relaxed state that the body returns to in homeostasis.

By itself, the mind's rebalancing act is astonishingly effective already. Gaze for thirty seconds at a bright light in the room or on your computer screen and close your eyes. You will see a retinal afterglow that then starts to fade. The time it takes the afterglow to go away entirely can be greater than a few minutes. The mind, however, cannot afford afterimages of thoughts: they would obscure the next thought. Consider the thousands of thoughts that run through your head in a week, or even a day, and how you are ready to receive each of them in flickering mental snapshots. The whole operation takes place literally at the speed of light—the speed of your brain's electrical signals.

TOTAL MEDITATION
Lesson 4: The Zero Point

Your mind hits a reset button the instant a thought registers. This is like the zero point of awareness. It's almost as if the mind erases the thought so a new thought can take its place. But unlike the Delete key on a computer, the zero point of the mind is alive, dynamic, and ready for anything that will come next. Ideally the zero point is vibrant and alert. You experience this ideal state when you are fresh, alert, optimistic, and ready for the next experience.

However, there are times when the zero point of the mind isn't at true rest. It returns instead to a state that is tired, dull, sunk in routine thoughts, and resistant to change. On a daily basis, we find ourselves somewhere in the middle of the best and worst the zero point has to offer. We don't feel mentally sluggish and fatigued, but neither are we open, curious, and fresh.

To illustrate what I mean, here are a few ways of noticing what it feels like when the zero point of the mind is less than ideal:

- Create irritating, distracting noise in your surroundings, which might mean turning up the volume on some music you dislike or setting your television to a channel with static. Sit with your eyes closed, and clear your mind.

Notice how hard it is to be quiet inside. The zero point can hardly be reached, and when it is, you still feel irritated.

- Now find a quiet, soothing setting where you feel relaxed. Close your eyes, take a few deep breaths, and quiet your mind. Notice how easily you reach the zero point. Even though thoughts come and go, they are not obscured by irritability or distraction.

- Experiment with how the zero point feels in various situations: in line at the post office; waiting to be seen at the doctor's; sitting around at the airport for a delayed flight; listening to a person you find boring; attending a tedious meeting at work.

Notice how easily the zero point is thrown off. This is due to the mind's inherent sensitivity. Your mind is trained to be attentive, picking up a wealth of information in every situation. This sensitivity is an enormous asset, but, at the same time, the piling up of information—particularly if it is unwelcome—makes it harder for the mind to return to the zero point with freshness and clarity.

Your mind wants to reset itself many times a minute to keep your thinking fresh, your attitude open, your mood optimistic. Such is Nature's design, but modern life works against Nature all the time. Quiet mind has become more difficult to reach, and in a society dominated by countless distractions and diversions, we look on a quiet mind as a rare experience. Perversely, many people prefer to eat in a crowded, noisy restaurant because they want constant stimulation.

The mind resists constant stimulation, which would wear us out like a vinyl record running with the needle digging into it all the time. This is also why we sometimes "space out" if we find ourselves in a situation in which there is too much going on around us. Except in cases of inner distress or external stressors, your thoughts will return to the zero point without any action on your part.

GOING INTO MEDITATION MODE

The tradition of meditation arose in order to launch from the zero point into a realm beyond everyday thoughts. Therefore, quiet mind isn't a goal in itself. It's a launchpad. In silence, all growth in consciousness occurs.

All the major meditation techniques correspond to various natural processes your mind goes through in returning to the zero point. You are actually recovering from some kind of imbalance that has temporarily thrown you out of equilibrium. In total meditation, we take advantage of all the mind's natural processes to address all imbalances together, not just one at a time. It helps to recognize how complete the mind's natural meditation mode really is and how often you go into it.

MINDFULNESS is the way your mind recovers from *distraction*. You are brought back into the present moment. The present is naturally where every cell in your body lives already. It is also where the mind wants to live, if you allow it to.

EXAMPLES:

- Your cell phone rings while you are driving. If you are mindful, you don't answer, keeping your focus in the here and now.

- You are at the doctor's, feeling worried about a potential medical problem. As the doctor discusses things with you, you notice that your mind is still preoccupied with worry. If you are mindful, you focus on what the doctor is saying and ask pertinent questions.

- You are on a date, and things aren't ideal. You notice less than desirable features in your date, and at the same time you wonder how you are coming off in their eyes. If you are mindful, you shoo away these distractions and experience the other person naturally, without second thoughts.

SELF-INQUIRY is the way your mind recovers from *habits*. By asking yourself, "Why am I doing this?" you bring conscious attention to a situation in which you have usually been ruled by habit, routine, obsessive behavior, knee-jerk reactions, and stagnant beliefs. Self-inquiry occurs when you notice repeated behavior and ask yourself about it.

EXAMPLES:

- You find yourself repeatedly asking your spouse or partner to help you with a household chore, only to have your request ignored or met with a lame excuse, such as "Sorry, I just forgot." Using self-inquiry, you ask yourself why you put yourself in the position of an adult talking to a child.

- You are easily tempted to order dessert at a restaurant even when you are full or are on a diet. With self-inquiry, you stop and ask yourself if this is really good for you. Since you know it isn't, why are you repeating this behavior?

- You complain about work all the time, and there are only short periods when things go right. With self-inquiry, you ask yourself why you remain in a job that makes you unhappy and whether you deserve better.

REFLECTION is the way your mind recovers from *thoughtlessness*. You regard your behavior, see what is self-defeating or troubling about it, and realize what is actually going on. The mind is naturally thoughtful when it reflects upon itself.

EXAMPLES:

- There's someone at work who rubs you the wrong way. You are getting fed up, but your coworkers don't seem to have the same problem with this person. So instead of focusing on the stress this person is causing you, you reflect on whether you are creating stress for them.

- You consider yourself a caring but vigilant parent. Recently your teenage daughter has become distant and secretive about what she is doing. You reflect on whether you have been hovering or whether she is acting like a normal teenager struggling to find the right boundaries.

- Your spouse or partner has lost the desire to maintain the sex life you enjoyed in the past. Your friends leap to the conclusion that your partner is having an affair, while you privately worry that you are no longer as desirable or attractive as before. On reflection you drop these assumptions, deciding to initiate changes in your love life that will satisfy both of you. If that doesn't work, you will reflect on what to do next.

CONTEMPLATION is the way your mind recovers from *confusion*. When faced with multiple choices, each with its pros and cons, you sort things out by contemplating the situation until you have a certain level of clarity. The mind naturally prefers clarity over confusion.

EXAMPLES:

- You have become irregular about going to church or have stopped altogether. Now your son is marrying a fundamentalist who keeps pressuring you about your faith. You want to keep peace in the family, but you don't have much lingering religious faith. So you contemplate how to convey your beliefs without making waves.

- You have a new boss who has made your job much more difficult in terms of pressure, deadlines, and his behavior. Do you stay there, try to fix it, or walk away? You contemplate and weigh the options.

- You are deeply moved about the problem of gun violence in this country. Everyone tells you that the gun lobby is too powerful to get sane gun regulation passed. You contemplate the value of following your conscience and pushing for new laws anyway, or whether the odds are so against you that such efforts are doomed.

CONCENTRATION IS the way your mind recovers from *pointlessness*. It is pointless to do a careless job, have careless opinions, or relate to other people in an unconcerned or arbitrary way. Such behaviors reflect an underlying belief that most things are pointless anyway, so why bother? By concentrating itself, the mind gets absorbed in something deeply enough that it has a point. This satisfies the mind's natural urge to find life meaningful.

EXAMPLES:

- One of your old friendships has become stale and routine, and your friend seems boring. Instead of leaving things at that, you concentrate on what you can do to rekindle your relationship.

- You have gotten good at your work, so good that it no longer challenges you. There's a risk that job will no longer be fulfilling. Before making the difficult decision to move on to a new job, you focus on how you can make your current job more meaningful and challenging.

- When you get up in the morning, you aren't eager for the day ahead. Things feel kind of blah. Instead of blaming your age, your spouse, your job, or life in general, you concentrate on inner change, asking what your life lacks and how to fill that lack through your own efforts.

PRAYER is the way your mind recovers from *helplessness*. By contacting a higher power, you are acknowledging a need for connection. Often we can feel isolated, alone, small, and lost.

Those are the qualities of helplessness, and for centuries humans have summoned God or the gods to bring a higher power into their life. The mind naturally wants to be rid of feeling powerless.

EXAMPLES:

- You have suffered a personal loss and feel depressed and lonely. To relieve this suffering you ask in prayer that it be resolved through grace or through a loving God.

- You witness a natural disaster somewhere in the world that brings untold misery to a huge number of people. Giving to charity doesn't feel like enough, so you pray to find a better way to help.

- You have a family member who has become addicted to drugs. All efforts to help have failed. A period in recovery always leads to a relapse. You pray that help can be found and ask that a higher power enters the picture to change it somehow.

QUIET MIND is the way your mind recovers from *overwork*. The mind is constantly processing daily life and its challenges, but when mental activity becomes burdensome, there is a risk of exhaustion, anxiety, and mental agitation. The mind naturally wants to be quiet when no activity is necessary. In peace and silence lie the simple contentment of existence and a renewed appetite for the next situation that demands a response.

EXAMPLES:

- At work you lash out at someone for being irresponsible. The person is upset, and afterward so are you. Before apologizing, you find a quiet place to regroup and let your mind rest.

- Your family has gotten used to your carrying a heavy load, and you are proud of how competent you are at this—everything you do is out of love. But you've been hiding a growing weariness. Before you discuss how others can do their share, you take time to relax and be quiet until you are ready to discuss things without feeling harassed inside.

- After a hard day at work, you're used to having a cocktail or beer, and recently your consumption has gone up. You realize that you can unwind more effectively by meditating or, at the very least, by relaxing for fifteen minutes before deciding if you really need a drink.

CONTROLLED BREATHING is the way your mind recovers from *stress*. *Stress* is a blanket term for an imbalanced state of mind and body under pressure. Breathing becomes rapid and irregular under stress. By taking a few deep breaths, sighing deeply, or falling asleep (a natural state of regular, relaxed breathing), your mind and body return to balance.

EXAMPLES:

- All examples come down to the same thing. When you feel stressed, check to see how you are breathing. Taking regular deep breaths for a few minutes meets the pressure with a relaxation response that clears your head and removes tension from your body.

BLISS is the way your mind recovers from *suffering*. The mind naturally prefers well-being to suffering, no matter how much we rationalize that certain forms of suffering are good for us. Bliss, joy, or ecstasy is a state of perfect happiness. It seems to arrive unpredictably, but we all have experienced it, and the mind wants to be there as much as possible. Bliss is a natural state. Suffering is an unnatural distortion, a kind of persistent bad vibration that destroys the mind's good vibrations.

EXAMPLES:

- Bliss is happiness beyond words, so it is different from feeling happy, which can often be described. To recognize the difference, search your memory for a time when you felt sudden joy without really knowing why. The more uncanny the feeling, the closer to bliss you came.

- If it isn't easy to recall an ecstatic moment, related feelings such as wonder and awe may be easier to grasp. See yourself before a landscape that filled you with the wonder of Nature—bliss is very close to that feeling.

- Bliss can be close to tears, too. Recall how you felt at seeing a newborn baby or child innocently at play or someone rising above their suffering. When these experiences overwhelm us, if the feeling they arouse is inspirational, it is close to bliss.

TOTAL MEDITATION
Lesson 5: Finding Your Center

Your mind already knows how to meditate. All you need to do is notice and take advantage. No matter what meditation practice you engage in, the process always involves centering. To be centered means to rest easily in your body, feeling quietly like yourself, with no demands or expectations. This is the departure point for everything else that can happen with total meditation. On the other hand, if you are not centered, nothing will happen in your meditation. Distraction is the hobgoblin of meditation, annoyingly pulling us away from what is most important.

It helps to recognize that centering occurs naturally outside meditation. You feel centered whenever you are serious and sincere. Speaking your own truth happens only when you are centered. An emotion expressed from the heart also comes from being centered.

Here is how to find your center anytime you want:

- Find a quiet place, close your eyes, and let your attention gently go to the center of your chest, in the region of the heart. Breathe easily and do nothing. You will sense that you are centered and quiet.

- Continue to do nothing, and your attention will start wandering again. Notice this and bring your attention back to your center.

Repeat the exercise as often as you like. Your aim is simply to notice the sensation of being centered. This sensation is the threshold to pure awareness, the steady state of consciousness.

To make use of what you've learned, go about your day, and pause if you happen to notice any of the following:

Feeling frazzled

Feeling distracted

Experiencing jumbled or racing thoughts

Feeling doubtful about making a decision

Feeling pressured

Worrying over time, money, or your health

Getting irritated or impatient

Fretting

Feeling bored

Whenever any of these very common responses begins, don't fight it. Instead, take a quiet moment with eyes closed to center yourself. Let awareness restore you to feeling steady, calm, in a place where you are no longer reacting to outside events. Don't force anything. If your attention wanders, gently bring it back to the center of your chest.

CONSCIOUSNESS IS "ALL OR ALL"

Some things in life are all-or-nothing propositions, like being pregnant, but most are not. You can live in the middle where "good enough" is found. Only consciousness is "all or all," a phrase that needs explaining.

When something is total, it cannot be divided up. There is only the whole thing. Consciousness is always present in every fiber of life, without exception. Because you have free will, you can push consciousness away, which we do all the time whenever we ignore what's good for us and instead choose to do what's bad for us. Habits push consciousness away. Rules push consciousness away. Anything that makes life mechanical pushes consciousness away, and yet consciousness remains unaffected.

The awakened life is totally conscious, which makes it the most natural way to live. Yet it is very hard for people to accept this concept. They like living by rules, for example, and when the rules are very strict, as they are for Orthodox Brahmins in Hinduism or Orthodox Jews, it is easy to feel superior because you follow so many dictates that the ordinary person would not be able to adhere to.

Total meditation opens a path to the awakened life, but first you have to want that life. Being aware all the time in every situation sounds strange and not necessarily good. What if you are aware all the time of your weight or your partner's shortcomings or of how little you actually know on any subject compared with a textbook writer? That's not what the awakened life is like, however. I cannot repeat too often that total awareness is the best way to live because consciousness is total already.

The body, as always, is the prefect touchstone for reality. Your body does more than rebalance itself through homeostasis—it also heals itself, and it does this all the time, not just when you feel sick or get injured. Thousands of times a day, irregular cells, including those that might be cancerous, are destroyed, and when they reach the end of their functional life, cells voluntarily die. The body is constantly vigilant, and this fact implies constant awareness.

As with so many other processes, the healing response is extremely complicated, and describing it fills textbooks without coming to the end of the subject. For our purposes, it is important to realize that consciousness is behind the actions your body takes, right down to the cellular level. A cell's intelligence tells it what to do. Its atoms and molecules would jiggle randomly like interstellar dust without consciousness. I think you will be convinced with an example taken from the immune system that can stand for the whole body.

One kind of white blood cell in your bloodstream, known as a phagocyte, is responsible for devouring invading microorganisms, while a second kind, known as a lymphocyte, recognizes and remembers any invader from the past—not just your past, either, but going back thousands, if not millions of years.

A white cell can stand for your entire body, because it has a visible and an invisible component. It's mesmerizing to watch through a microscope as a killer T cell, a type of lymphocyte, surrounds, engulfs, and devours an unwanted bacterium or virus, but it is the invisible intelligence of lymphocytes that makes the entire immune system viable. We depend on almost perfect memory from the immune system. Your ability to recognize a face is akin to a lymphocyte's recognizing the viruses that cause measles and mumps. By remembering that you had measles and mumps as a child, the lymphocyte protects you from ever having them again.

Medical science is baffled by the occasions when one of two things goes wrong: Either a harmless particle is mistakenly recognized as an enemy, which is how allergies develop. Or immune cells begin to attack the body's own cells, creating an autoimmune disorder (of which there are around fifty, including lupus and rheumatoid arthritis).

Allergies and autoimmune disorders have been on a sharp increase in recent decades, particularly in developed countries, and no one can explain why. This is because, to date, the immune system has been studied exclusively for its physical side, with minimal knowledge about its invisible intelligence. It's as if we understood Einstein's work by examining how much chalk he used on the blackboard. Naturally, we look instead at the meaning of what he wrote with his chalk, but that's not possible with a white cell, whose intelligence is hidden. Its intelligence is known only by observing what the cell can remember.

If you delve deeper, the mystery of memory in the immune system is the same as the mystery of memory, period. In the brain, memory is spread across several regions, including the hippocampus, a part of the brain that is important for consolidating information (the name refers to the Greek for seahorse, whose shape the hippocampus was thought to resemble). In a famous surgical disaster in the 1950s, a man's hippocampus was surgically cut away in the hope of curing his epileptic seizures, and there was some improvement. But the man completely lost his memory, making him the unique object of study for the ensuing decades until his death. A total absence of memory makes every experience new but also empty. The man had no relationships, for example. His doctor would have to introduce himself every time he walked into the room, even if he had been absent for barely a minute.

Knowing the location of memory is helpful for mapping purposes, but the structure of the hippocampus tells us about as much about memory as if you knew where your smartphone was but didn't know how to operate it. Since the visible, or physical, side of memory offers so little understanding, we must turn to its invisible side. What do we know about memory? Tons, but it is all subjective.

We know that memories can be recalled but also arise on their own.

We know that memories, if vivid enough, bring back the emotions of the original circumstances that created the memory, often with an intense recollection of pain.

We know that some memories are accurate, while others are faulty. The mind even produces completely false memories about the past, or merges several incidents together.

This knowledge comes to us simply by using memory, but unlike the memory in a computer, which is mechanically stored as digits of 1 and 0, human memory somehow has a life of its own. We are often used by our memories instead of the other way around. By this, I mean that memories force us to relive painful experiences we would rather forget. They remind us of our past failures and limitations. They keep alive old grudges and offenses we are unable to forgive. At the most basic level, we lack a method for erasing unwanted memories, which is one reason people find it necessary to go into denial—a willful kind of forgetting.

The fact is that almost everything the body does is controlled by the background consciousness that is ever present, intelligent, and vigilant. We know some things through personal experience that science is baffled by. Memory is a glaring example, and so is healing. But there is no lesson taught in medical school that isn't confronted by mysteries. In my own field of endocrinology, for example, it was thought as late as 1995 that hormones were secreted only by the endocrine glands like the thyroid, pancreas, and adrenal glands. Then it was discovered that fat cells secret a hormone known as leptin, which controls the sensation of satiation, or having enough to eat. If this wasn't surprising enough, it was then discovered that endocrine hormones are secreted everywhere in the body. Your bones, for example, secrete a special hormone, and your skin is now known to be the body's major source of hormones of every kind.

A further blow to the field came when it was discovered that each hormone has more than one function, and often the functions bear no relationship to one another. Testosterone, for example, isn't simply the male sex hormone. It exists in women, too, and its functions include sex drive, bone mass, fat distribution, muscle size and strength, and red blood cell production. In short, our hormones, like the healing response, require total knowledge of everything the body is doing and needs to do.

MEDITATION ISN'T THE SAME AS THINKING

My shorthand for consciousness is that it is everywhere and everything. Yet our thoughts, the most obvious example of consciousness, are not always aware. You didn't think your immune system into existence; you don't heal a cut by thinking about it. Trying to understand consciousness by thinking, in fact, is the very worst way to understand it. Only direct experience of consciousness leads to understanding. That's why meditation and thinking are nowhere near the same thing.

Thinking can be so wrong that it blocks the natural rebalancing the mind is designed for. Let me illustrate what I mean through a first-person account found at a personal website by Joey Lott, a man with no medical credentials who discovered, through years of trial and error, what he calls "the cure for anxiety":

> I lived for the first 32 years of my life in anxiety. It grew to the point at which I was in panic all day and all night ... for many years. I felt like an electric current was going through my body, electrify-

ing my nerves, causing me to feel unable to find
any ease or okayness.

There is no consensus about what causes chronic anxiety.
A natural response—fear in the face of danger—becomes free
floating, no longer attached to any actual threat. In Lott's case,
the symptoms were complex and overlapping.

> From the age of 11 I struggled with OCD and an-
> orexia. In shame, I hid and avoided. I starved
> myself and over-exercised. I washed my hands
> dozens of times a day. . . . I tried to blank out un-
> wanted thoughts and images. I tried to do social
> things only to find myself running back to the rela-
> tive safety of my home. But even my home wasn't
> safe. I would lie awake at night in terror, imagining
> all kinds of things that might be happening.

In frustration Lott sought professional help, along with a
wide range of self-remedies, none of which was a cure.

> I failed so completely to make things better (even
> after years of therapy, meditation, yoga, affirma-
> tions, breathwork, prayer, hundreds of self-help
> books, countless workshops, and on and on) that
> eventually I grew hopeless. Nothing could help
> me, I believed. I thought I was broken.

The cure he ultimately discovered is a form of "not doing," to use a Buddhist term. However, it was the experience, not the terminology, that was key. Lott realized that his anxiety was rooted in thought itself, in the mind's constant attempt to attack anxiety in self-defeating ways. The cure, he declares,

> is completely counterintuitive, because it is *not* about getting rid of unwanted symptoms. It is not about getting *rid* of anxiety. It is not about defeating anxiety or breaking free of anxiety.

It is about actually discovering directly what anxiety is and welcoming it home.

The method Lott has in mind is to stop resisting anxiety in any way. He maintains that resistance—along with every attempt to get rid of anxiety—is the cause of anxiety. Instead of getting entangled in so much mental activity, Lott decided to bypass all of it:

> The essential cure for anxiety is . . . the direct meeting of the experience. Not trying to get rid of it, calm it, change it, fix it, solve it, or anything else.
> How does one go about direct meeting?
> Simple. Do nothing.

Words can easily get in the way, and few who suffer from anxiety, whether in mild, moderate, or severe form, would accept that to do nothing is a cure. I think what has happened here is due to the mind's ability to heal and rebalance itself. Lott found a way to allow this process to unfold, and for him the secret was to confront his anxiety directly. Other people might find this too frightening to consider. But, as a general principle, healing is fostered when we learn to get out of the way as much as possible. Picking at a wound will only make it worse. Refusing to rest when you have the flu will prolong the symptoms.

Lott is conscientious about telling his readers that the various methods he tried, such as mindfulness and meditation, can help with anxiety. With the fervor of someone who has healed himself, he believes he has found the real cure. Needless to say, there is no accepted medical model for it, and, as a physician, I must add that I am not endorsing such a cure. Lott found, with himself and other people he was later in contact with, that it is possible to "do nothing"—that is, to simply be aware of what was happening. It worked for him.

Even to recognize a fleeting experience of this kind might require a coach, as Lott freely admits. The mind is habituated to pay attention to its thoughts, and it is all but impossible to *not* pay attention. Anxiety grows the more you think about it. To break this vicious circle, one can start by paying less attention to the symptoms, not dwelling on them. If you get used to not obsessing over any experience, however painful or distracting, in time your attention gets attracted to self-awareness instead. Eventually the mind returns to a state of normal balance, which is where healing comes from.

There's an important lesson here about the difference between thinking and meditating. Meditating aligns the mind with balance and healing. Total consciousness is allowed to do its work without the interference of worry, doubt, self-pity, hopelessness, and helplessness. Even when we don't give in to these detriments, they nibble around the edges of any chronic condition. A "condition" can be medical, but a bad relationship or a boring job are also conditions that throw us out of balance. The longer the condition persists, the worse it becomes.

Lott gained access to a hidden ability in his own awareness. That's what meditation does—not the partial meditation that failed him, but a process that becomes second nature in daily life. True meditation is simply a reminder by the mind of its role as healer. We remember something crucial that should never be forgotten again.

TOTAL MEDITATION
Lesson 6: Expanded Awareness

You can experiment with the mind's healing abilities through a simple exercise in self-awareness.

1. Find a quiet place where you won't be disturbed for 5 or 10 minutes.
2. Close your eyes and let your attention freely go to a place of discomfort in your body. If you have mental pain instead—a worry, for example, or any persistent feeling that is bothering you—let it come to mind.
3. Focus lightly on the bodily discomfort or painful thought for a few seconds, then take your attention away from it. Focus on the outline of your body instead. Feel the air around you, the temperature on your skin, and the sensation of your whole body.
4. Return to your discomfort or painful thought, then once again expand your awareness away from that sensation to your whole body. Repeat several times.
5. Now expand a little farther. Feel your discomfort or painful thought, then expand your awareness to the room around you. Listen to any sounds, then visualize your awareness

expanding like a balloon to fill the room. Repeat several times.

6. Finally, expand your awareness everywhere.
   Feel your discomfort or painful thought, then
   sense your awareness going beyond the walls
   of the room, out of the building, and steadily
   growing until it has expanded beyond all
   boundaries.

7. Sit quietly for a moment, then open your eyes.

For most people, the bodily discomfort or painful
thought they began with will have diminished, sometimes remarkably. Extreme, persistent pain and anguish
can vanish. One session isn't a permanent cure, naturally, but this exercise is really about learning *not* to pay
attention.

Any kind of pain demands attention. It is up to you
whether to passively give in. If you do, you will aggravate
the pain, like the way your tongue will worry about a sore
tooth or cold sore by constantly touching it over and over.

To get out of this automatic reaction, you can consciously move your awareness wherever you want it to
go. That's what you are learning to do in this exercise. It's
a perfect example of how to free yourself from a stuck
response simply by taking control over your awareness.

3

Let Your Body Guide You

There's a critical misconception that needs clearing up. It's the idea that meditation is "all in your head." People want practical results from meditating. This is understandable. Meditation can improve your life for the better by helping you to become less anxious and more focused. It offers the experience of quiet mind. Currently, the attentive state known as mindfulness is all the rage. But the mind isn't separate from the body, which is always involved. For instance, to lose the lingering effects of old, unwanted memories, the brain must no longer retrieve them.

Every sensation you have comes through the central nervous system, including the sensations associated with love, peace, and even the presence of God. Extraordinary as any spiritual experiences might be, they are still physical reactions in the nervous system. To see meditation as just something mental is to misunderstand how total meditation really *works*.

The mind-body connection merges physical and mental activity. The mind responds to the body at the same instant the body responds to the mind. This fact, which seems obvious today, used to be adamantly resisted. Few Western doctors "believed in" the mind-body connection when it was first proposed. They insisted—as some still do—that only the physical side mattered. I remember my frustration when senior physicians in Boston would scoff at the notion that the body could be affected by meditating. I had one encounter with a Harvard Medical School professor who so thoroughly dismissed the mind-body connection that I blurted out, "For heaven's sake, how do you think you move your toes?" He didn't budge.

Such denials seems like ancient history, and yet they linger in the widespread notion that what we consider the self, the individual person, is simply a creation of brain activity. This is the new flashpoint of disagreement. The average person might rightfully look upon such controversy as irrelevant to their own life, but it isn't. Beyond the mind-body connection, vital questions demand answers.

Does the brain create the mind? If so, are we just robots at the beck and call of the brain?

Is the pursuit of expanded or higher awareness a fantasy? If you have no self except for squiggles of brain activity, there's zero likelihood you have a higher self, so why even bother meditating, praying, or being kind to your neighbor? You are simply fostering an illusion.

But can the mind really override the brain? The act of mind over matter meets with skepticism and even ridicule in the "brain only" camp, even though there is copious scientific evidence to suggest that you are in more control of your brain than you realize. If you pile up so many bills that you begin to worry about your finances, your brain chemistry changes. Your anxious emotion triggered these changes. It makes no sense to say that you are worrying because your brain made you anxious— your mind started the process when you saw your credit card statement.

Still, many of us are convinced that we live solely in a material world. On many fronts, including science, philosophy, and the mass media, the "brain only" position seems to have won. Few people fully support the possibility that consciousness could be independent of the brain. Even less do people accept what this book proposes, that consciousness creates the brain. How can a nonphysical entity go about building neurons in the first place? The mystery is solved once you realize that we are not separated into mind and body. We are one thing: the bodymind, which unites the two.

TOTAL MEDITATION
Lesson 7: The Bodymind

Brain activity can be seen on a functional MRI or a CT scan, but thoughts cannot. Clearly the two activities are connected, but *connected* is too weak a term. Brain and mind are indivisible. It isn't a matter of which came first. The bodymind is one thing, and because it operates as one, it has always existed as one.

If you want proof, here's a simple demonstration of mind and body being inseparable:

- Close your eyes and imagine a bright yellow lemon with a kitchen knife beside it.
- See the knife cut the lemon in half, watching drops of lemon juice spritz into the air. At some point in this visualization, you will begin to salivate involuntarily (I did while writing the exercise down).

This is a classic example of the mind-body connection. But what is often missed is that the brain doesn't know the difference between an imaginary lemon and a real one. The brain triggers your salivary glands in either case. Yet your mind does know the difference, because you are not your brain.

You are *using* your brain, and doing so with complete reliance on the fact that the brain and the mind react simultaneously and almost instantly to each other. It is impossible to locate where one ends and the other begins.

HEALING THE DISCONNECT

In hindsight, it seems peculiar that anyone had to discover a so-called mind-body connection, because it is impossible to be a person without it. It's rather like "discovering" that Fuji apples are red and sweet. The experience of that particular type of apple includes those qualities. An apple wouldn't be an apple without them.

Yet there was a practical reason for needing to discover the mind-body connection, having to do with the troubling state known in psychology as dissociation. *Dissociation* is broadly defined as "a wide array of experiences from mild detachment from immediate surroundings to more severe detachment from physical and emotional experiences."

Doctors and therapists treat dissociation at the extreme end of the dissociation spectrum, where mind and body are severely disconnected. Anorexia, for example, involves a disastrous disconnect between a mental obsession over losing weight and the physical evidence of an emaciated body that desperately needs food. A young woman might look at herself in the mirror and see someone grossly obese when, in fact, she weighs eighty pounds and is slowly dying of malnutrition.

Dissociation is also evident when a person goes into shock and bodily sensation goes numb. Someone who has just been in a serious car crash on a cold winter's night might be shivering in shock without the slightest mental recognition of being cold. It takes an outsider to wrap a blanket around them; they are in too much shock to do it for themselves.

Dissociation poses a mystery far deeper than its medical implications. Pain can be numbed by detaching yourself consciously, the very opposite of going into shock. This occurs in the spiritual state of detachment. Why are anorexia and bulimia maladies, shock a state of acute numbness, and detachment a spiritual goal? We have to look deeper into the bodymind to understand these differences.

Let's begin with the extraordinary experience of the South African writer and teacher Michael Brown. Brown was a music journalist who suddenly developed a very uncommon neurological disorder known as Horton's syndrome, which is rarely diagnosed in people under fifty. "This condition," Brown writes, "which started in 1987, manifested as multiple daily occurrences of excruciating agony." Severe inflammation of arteries in the brain results in so-called cluster headaches. Brown's case was an extreme example, and for almost ten years he found no relief. He tried prescription medications, went to native African medicine men, and consulted all manner of healers. His desperate plight caused one of the country's leading neurosurgeons to declare that Brown was a candidate for either a lifelong addiction to painkillers or ending his pain through suicide.

"In 1994," Brown writes, "after years of pursuing endless modalities that led nowhere, I was confronted with the possibility that nothing and nobody 'out there' could alleviate my suffering. My options at this point were either to *check out*—or *check in*."

Choosing the second option proved to be decisive. Brown experimented with different self-induced mental states. He discovered that his pain lessened if he could bring himself into what he terms "a high personal energy frequency." He had made a mind-body connection on his own. "This was the first whisper of what I now call present moment awareness."

A dramatic breakthrough followed in the Arizona desert in 1996. Brown attended a sweat lodge ceremony led by a Native American guide. Such ceremonies involve intense heat, sweating, chanting, and drumming. Ordinary states of awareness are put under extreme pressure for a few hours. When Brown emerged, crawling out of the sweat lodge on his hands and knees, he suddenly experienced a dramatic shift inside.

"As I stood there in the cool night air, everything in and around me vibrated with life, as if I had just been born. . . . I stood by the fire in reverent silence, remaining long into the night, feeling warm blood flowing through my veins, crisp breath massaging my lungs, and the comforting rhythm of my heartbeat." He terms this his first experience of Presence, or *beingness*. He "showed up" in his own life, which Brown describes as follows: "I felt physically present, mentally clear, emotionally balanced, and vibrationally 'in tune.'"

As told in his book, *The Presence Process*, this breakthrough led to Brown's gaining control over his neurological condition, and his experience in the Arizona desert underscores that "showing up" in your own life—in other words, becoming much more aware—requires the body to show up as well. What is this mysterious Presence that Brown encountered? He takes almost a religious attitude toward it, but I think the answer is simple: when you are present, there is an encounter with Presence.

Not every person who enters a sweat lodge, or tries another intense spiritual practice, comes out with an experience of being totally present. We drift in and out of awareness, and as we do, this creates the unpredictability of Presence. In other words, we are typically in a state of dissociation, or disconnect. Sometimes it takes a severe jolt to make this apparent. There is a tradition both East and West of placing the body under intense stress, which can cause a sudden snap into full awareness. Soldiers have experienced this on the battlefield, when a state of fear and apprehension is transformed into sensations of total awareness. These sensations include

A feeling of physical lightness or even weightlessness

Heightened colors and sounds

Intense awareness of breathing and heartbeat

A tingling energy in the body

Total relaxation

Euphoria

What is seen in soldiers, extreme athletes, or victims of trauma is that awareness can dramatically click into a higher state of consciousness. This, however, doesn't lead to the conclusion that we should punish our bodies with stress, go to war, or seek extreme physical conditions. People who make a habit of high-stress living might hack into a temporary state of altered consciousness, but it is much more likely that they are becoming adrenaline junkies, not yogis. Heightened awareness isn't tense, excited, and physically exhausting in the aftermath—these are all hallmarks of an adrenaline rush. The aftereffects of an episode of higher consciousness are, in contrast, relaxed and blissful.

Having experienced a dramatic shift in consciousness, Michael Brown tried to bring his altered state under control so that it could be repeated at will. One of his key practices in "the Presence process," as he calls his program, is an extended practice of controlled breathing involving various detailed steps and a great deal of discipline. Yogis have practiced similar controlled breathing for many centuries. I doubt, however, that such sustained discipline is suitable in everyday life.

But Brown also came to the same conclusion I've been stressing in these pages. Namely, when Presence appears, it happens naturally and without effort. You can't force it. You can prepare the way, however, which is what we do in total meditation. It will always be true, I believe, that so-called peak experiences arrive on their own schedule. You can try to find them, but it is far more likely that they will find you. This isn't a frustrating trick of Nature.

Consciousness knows us better than we know ourselves.

Presence, or a peak experience, transforms a person when it is time for transformation. The good news is that the most valuable experiences, including euphoria and bliss, occur because there is a time for them in everyone's life.

In total meditation, the goal is to move the needle ahead on the spectrum, making steady progress every day. This might not be as spectacular as a sudden burst of awakening or as exciting as parachuting out of an airplane. But it lasts, because your entire being—body, mind, emotions, thoughts, desires, and relationships—becomes part of a natural development. States of disconnect we accepted as normal are knitted back into the harmony of the bodymind as it was meant to be.

TOTAL MEDITATION

Lesson 8: Feeling Your Way

There are two basic paths we take through life: thinking and feeling. Rational thought is highly prized in an age of science and technology, but in everyday life, all kinds of feelings intervene. People assume they are dealing with their life rationally, but for everyone there's a mixture of thinking and feeling. This mixture is confusing and needs to be straightened out if you want to make your way through life consciously, in full awareness.

To think your way through life appeals to rationalists, but they are fooling themselves. Feeling is always a part of every experience, every decision, every life choice. Here are some examples of how this works:

- Think of a food you hate (an American president made headlines by hating broccoli). See yourself putting a bite of this food in your mouth. It could be snails, a raw oyster, or boiled cabbage. Try to taste it as if you loved it instead. You can't, because its taste is cemented to your feeling about it.

- Put yourself in the place of a homeless person living with small children on the street. Visualize the situation—no doubt you've observed something similar in real life. Imagine that a stranger walks up to you and hands you $1,000 in cash. You thank them profusely, but then they laugh scornfully and snatch the money back. Can you see the situation without any emotion? This is a dramatic example of how everything we see comes with an interpretation at the level of feeling.

- Imagine that you are on a long hike in the mountains and lose track of time. Now it is dark, the temperature is falling fast, and you must get back to camp. In pitch blackness you reach a drop-off, almost stumbling over it. You vaguely remember that the drop isn't far, maybe two feet. On the other hand, if you've become lost, the drop-off could be a hundred feet. There is no turning back. Can you deal with the situation without feeling anxious? Few people could.

The point of these observations is that we all *feel* our way through life far more than we realize. We assume that we are thinking logically from one decision to another. In reality, how we feel is much more dominant. The ancients used to believe that the heart was the seat of intelligence, and in that they really weren't wrong. *Feeling has its own deep intelligence.*

It is limiting and often damaging to overlook that fact. Someone will say that they feel too much. They always lead with the heart, for example, and because of this they get their heart broken a lot. Yet as often as not, love is lost by overthinking and not paying enough attention to feelings with an attitude of trust. I think heartfulness is just as present as mindfulness.

In the end, learning how to feel your way through life offers the best hope of happiness and success. *Feeling occurs in the whole bodymind*, which gives us a practical reason to unite body and mind rather than trying to keep them separate.

THE WISDOM OF THE BODY

In many ways the body and not the mind should be the measure of what meditation can achieve. By *body*, I'm not referring to the brain specifically, although its functions extend to every cell in the body, which implies that everything we attribute to the brain should be present everywhere, and so it is. Your immune system, for example, functions with a complete memory of every disease you and your ancestors have ever had. This memory goes into action whenever invading bacteria, viruses, and fungi appear in the bloodstream. Just as you recognize whether a face is familiar or unfamiliar, so do immune cells. They attack familiar pathogens as soon as they appear. If the invader has taken a new genetic identity, which happens with fast-mutating cold viruses (this winter's strain of colds and flu are new faces on the block, as is the far more catastrophic newcomer COVID-19), your immune system quickly learns all about this new identity and develops new antibodies to fight it.

In a few sentences. I've outlined *four aspects of consciousness that belong not only to the brain but to every cell: memory, recognition, learning, and creativity.* If we weren't misled by meditation being "all in your head," it would be obvious that consciousness is a global property inherent in life itself. But the story has another, deeper plotline. By themselves, the qualities of consciousness are very general. Memory in a white cell shares memory with heart, liver, and brain cells. This is a fixed trait, or quality of consciousness. Life is always moving and changing, however, so memory must run alongside, constantly adapting to the next invading pathogen, but also to the next place a wound needs healing, the next renegade cell that might be precancerous, the next person's name you need to remember, and so on. The tasks of memory are endless, indeed infinite.

That's how totality works. By adapting to life's infinite experiences, consciousness must be infinite just to catch up, as it were. In reality, consciousness leads the way, and the prime leadership role is given to the body. You can be in deep sleep or in a coma, and your cells will still be fully conscious and aware. This awareness has its own wisdom. Certain principles of the body have been tested for millions of years, ever since the first multicelled organisms appeared on Earth, and these principles now govern our existence as a bodymind.

WISDOM IN ACTION

Your body is filled with its own wisdom, putting in action the most fundamental principles of consciousness. We get visible proof of this beginning at the level of cells:

Cells cooperate with one another for the greater good.

Vastly different organs understand and accept how other organs work.

Healing is a response that calls upon the whole community of cells.

Conflict has been banished in favor of peaceful coexistence.

The outer world is constantly sensed and adapted to.

New experiences are met with creative responses.

The fact that these principles apply automatically doesn't mean they do not announce themselves to you. You feel your way through life, in fact, by receiving messages about your own behavior as sensed by your body. These are nonverbal messages delivered in chemical form. They can be roughly divided into two categories: warnings of trouble and signs of well-being.

WARNINGS OF TROUBLE: pain, physical discomfort, tightness and tension in muscles, headache, lower back pain and stiffness, nausea, insomnia, lethargy, fatigue.

Although patients show up at the doctor's to have these warnings treated as medical conditions, it is just as important to listen to them as actual communications to be heeded. For example, each warning has psychological implications. Nausea can come from eating the wrong food but can also come from nervousness, ranging from mild butterflies in the stomach to paralyzing stage fright. Lethargy and fatigue are signs of stress. The stress can be physical, like heavy physical labor, or mental, like the pressure of a deadline at work. Reading what your body is trying to tell you allows you to feel your way to healing earlier rather than later.

SIGNS OF WELL-BEING: lightness, energy, physical flexibility, good muscle tone, sound sleep, good digestion, absence of colds and flu, bright eyes, dynamism.

These signs are the opposite of warnings of trouble. In a consumer society, products are peddled that supposedly give more energy and vitality, but, in reality, well-being is the normal resting state of your body. The signals you receive are like the quiet humming of a perfectly tuned car, except that this analogy leaves out the living nature of well-being. Again there is a psychological component. Well-being brings a sense of optimism, contentment, safety, stability, and openness to new experiences.

Once you absorb how full and complete the wisdom of the body is, it's hard not to blush at our failure, both personal and social, to match it. The peaceful coexistence that is only a tiny portion of the body's wisdom has been achieved only by fits and starts in human history. Unfortunately, the mutual understanding that different organs have with one another is, at the level of society, beset with prejudice, suspicion, and hatred.

What went wrong? If the bodymind is a seamless whole, and

if the body is so wise, why do many of us experience insomnia, anxiety, digestive problems, and stress-related disorders? There must be a disconnect somewhere. Stress is one of the chief causes of disconnect in the first place. A 2019 Yale psychological study uncovered that student stress had doubled in the preceding decade. Searching for the cause of this dramatic rise, one can point to the increasing lack of quiet mental time free of distraction.

Although far short of a full-blown stress response, perpetually looking at your smartphone for texts and e-mail puts the bodymind on constant alert, which is no different, as far as your involuntary nervous system is concerned, from being in a state of wariness for danger. There are larger issues for students, such as the crushing burden of college debt, estimated at a staggering $1.47 trillion at the end of 2018. Such debt cascades into pressure to get good grades, hold a part-time job, and at the same time discover a financially secure occupation as quickly as possible. These macro-stresses, as they are termed by Dr. Rangan Chatterjee, a physician who specializes in stress, are actually not as important in the total picture as micro-stresses.

College debt and the pressure to perform didn't double in the last decade. But perpetual distraction, through video games as well as texting and e-mails, has become a way of life. The bodymind's natural state is to cope with stress and then return to balance as quickly as possible. Keep up a steady stream of such micro-stresses, which might hardly be noticeable to a smartphone addict, and in short order, Dr. Chatterjee says, you will have unwittingly approached your personal stress threshold.

All it takes, he points out, is to wake up and immediately

consult your messages—which might contain three work-related issues—before you have even had a cup of coffee. Your body-mind goes on alert, and if you encounter micro-stresses around the breakfast table, such as forgetting that you promised to take your daughter to band practice, followed by a few added micro-stresses on your commute to work, you will be close to your stress threshold the minute you arrive at the office. The result is impatience, irritability, distraction, and the likelihood that the next text leads to a blowup over something totally trivial.

The disconnect I've just described is what meditation seeks to repair. The direction of the repair work isn't a mystery—the body naturally guides us through early warnings of trouble on one hand and signs of well-being on the other. Heeding these signals is central to leading a conscious life. When you go into meditation mode, your mind is returning to a state of balance that mirrors the body's state of balance.

However, meditation in itself isn't sufficient to heal the state of disconnect, because of the divided self. The existence of bad habits, old conditioning, negative emotions, fixed beliefs, and all the rest of the apparatus we carry around in our psyche indicates a much deeper alienation. We war against one another and against ourself. We don't know what is good for us, and when we do, there's no guarantee we will act accordingly. The state of denial may be effective in some cases, but eventually fatigue, frustration, depression, anxiety, self-defeat, and self-judgment break through one way or another.

We need to realize that only consciousness can fully repair the disconnect, and it must be total consciousness, because mind and body have suffered together and need to heal together. Well-being is a state of wholeness, and your life cannot be whole until the bodymind is whole. Achieving total consciousness may, at this point in the book, sound impossible, but stay with me and you'll see that total consciousness is not only possible, it is a natural state.

If your body meditates along with your mind, that's a good working definition of totality. One of the first findings about meditation back in the 1970s showed that alpha wave activity increases in the brain during meditation. Alpha waves are a frequency range of brain activity that organize in sync. They can be detected by hooking a subject up for an EEG (electroencephalogram) and, in fact, were discovered by the inventor of the EEG, the German neurologist Hans Berger.

Ocean waves out at sea are disorganized, rising and falling at random, but the brain doesn't scramble its electrical activity into chaotic noise or static. Once brainwave activity was discovered—other EEG measurements revealed beta, gamma, theta, and delta waves, each sending a signal on its own frequency, like separate radio stations—a fund of information was gained. To a brain researcher, alpha waves are "neural oscillations in the frequency range of 8–12 Hz arising from the synchronous and coherent electrical activity of thalamic pacemaker cells in humans."

This information, however, tells us nothing about the mystery of alpha waves. Why did our brains evolve to produce them? They must serve a purpose; otherwise, they would belong to the category of evolutionary changes that vanished in prehistory because, from a Darwinian point of view, they were useless. Alpha waves are physically useful in regard to what they indicate the bodymind is doing: relaxing.

Alpha waves appear when you close your eyes and rest but are not tired or asleep (a second type of alpha wave occurs during REM, or dream, sleep). In itself, this phenomenon doesn't seem like anything special; all creatures need to rest and sleep. In fact, there are states of human awareness beyond relaxation that (so far as we know) only we possess and in which alpha waves dominate. These states include:

Smoothly flowing thoughts

Being alert in the moment

Meditation

Creative activity

Stable mood, decreased depression

Why are alpha waves increasing during these very human activities? It's uncertain. Your visual cortex takes a rest when you close your eyes. Is that a prelude to starting a creative activity? That's only a guess, because wiggly lines on an EEG are too crude to suggest, even remotely, what a person is getting ready to do. But anyone who has taken up amateur painting as a creative hobby can testify that it is relaxing.

Unlike drowsiness, the relaxed state indicated by alpha waves is quite alert. Some researchers have deemed alpha waves "the motor that drives the power of now." It isn't contradictory to be relaxed and alert at the same time—meditation brings on this state, in fact. Only human beings are aware that the power of now exists, and we have spent centuries pondering how to use it.

Trying to make the brain responsible for the infinite variety of human activity will always prove frustrating. When you do something new and creative, the entire bodymind obeys your intention. Creativity as a brain phenomenon would be like a radio producing a new Beethoven symphony. Neurons cannot be creators: creativity takes a mind that goes into a special state physically indicated by increased alpha waves. Let's say that Leonardo da Vinci decides one morning to paint the portrait of an elusive and beautiful young woman who became known as Mona Lisa. Once he picks up his palette, he muses over color, design, form, and artistic technique.

If Leonardo were alive today, we could spot the alpha waves on an EEG as he entered a creative mood, and if neuroscience one day makes a complete map of the brain's entire circuitry, we conceivably could know, nerve cell by nerve cell, what was happening as the *Mona Lisa* was born. It's hard for people to realize, however, that such a map in no way would tell us anything about the *Mona Lisa* as a work of art, because a botched painting by a total duffer also comes from the same brain activity. Art isn't in an alpha wave. It is in the consciousness that happens to induce alpha waves. The same setup occurs in countless other activities, whose value may be creative or merely relaxed.

TOTAL MEDITATION

Lesson 9: "I Am"

The bodymind is a fine concept that remains a concept until you translate it into your own experience. This is a tricky business. We are used to taking different roads for mental and physical experiences. If your palms are cold and sweaty, that condition takes place down a different road from the thought "I am going on a first date." Yet obviously the two belong together if a first date, or anything else, makes you feel extremely nervous.

How can we unite the two roads into one? Here's a method that connects body and mind by a simple maneuver, which is not to take any road at all, physical or mental. You constantly experience the bodymind without the words *body* or *mind* coming into play. Instead there is simply "I am": the experience of your sense of self. You don't need to pinch yourself to know you are awake. Likewise, you don't need to remind yourself in any way that your sense of self is always present.

Let's see how this works in practice.

- Look around the room and out the window to see whatever strikes your eye. Listen for sounds in your surroundings. Touch the roof of your mouth with your tongue to experience its texture and any flavors you might detect. Smell anything your nose happens to notice.

- Now shut your eyes and repeat the same sequence by imagining sights, sounds, textures, tastes, and smells.

At any given moment, you are entangled in these sensations, and they are not separate. They mingle into one sensation, the total experience of being here and now. "I am" is whatever sensation you are identifying with at the moment, sometimes singling out a sight or a thought, sometimes just mingling with the whole sensorium (a good example would be the experience of lying on a beach under the sun with a breeze and the sound of the waves taking you in together).

As the sensorium moves this way and that, "I am" pays attention. You are ready for the next sensation or thought. If you look closely, however, you will recognize that "I am" isn't really a chameleon. It takes on the color of a leaf, the fragrance of a rose, the texture of sandpaper, and so on. But all this occurs in an open space, the space of consciousness.

Consciousness is the space in which everything happens. Sights, sounds, textures, tastes, and smells pass through the space, but the space itself remains unchanged, the way an airport doesn't change when thousands of people pass through it every day.

When you grasp that "I am" is whole, free from thinking "I am my body" or "I am my mind," a great change occurs. You find that you can live in this unbounded space of "I am" quite easily. In fact, it is the natural place to be. A good example is body image. If you think "I am my body," the image you see in the mirror will mostly likely not be ideal. You will experience judgment about the image you see, and from this starting point you might vow to go to the gym, eat less, look into anti-aging products, and so on.

But if you don't focus on an image in the mirror, which runs up against images in your mind about how you should look and what is perfect and how short of perfection you are, reality then has nothing to do with images of any kind. Close your eyes, and you are sensing either warnings of trouble or signs of well-being. Nothing else really matters. Images come and go, as do all passing sensations. But in the open space of "I am," these transient experiences are just passing scenery. The real you is a passenger watching the scenery go by. Your attention wanders all over the scenery without your awareness wandering. Your awareness stays where it has always been, in "I am," without judgment. This absence of judgment is very liberating, which is why it is one of the major goals of total meditation.

WHO'S IN CHARGE?

Your brain has no bias for or against any state of mind. It obediently transforms itself according to what is demanded. The disconnect between mind and body, however, has a strong and lasting effect inside the brain. Worrying about money might make you feel a tightening in your chest and make you lose your appetite. Once the worries are over, those parts of the bodymind go back to their normal state. If you are a habitual worrier, however, you have altered pathways in your brain over time. Unless these pathways born of habit are changed, your brain becomes a coconspirator in your worry—the same would go for any mental state that persists long enough to have a strong effect on brain functioning, such as depression.

Fortunately, the brain is self-transforming. Sadness normally dissipates on its own without you making a move to improve your mood. Your brain is literally transformed when your mood changes from dark to light (or vice versa). How does it do this? There are some mysteries here that only consciousness can solve.

The brain isn't like a car, which runs only if you turn the ignition on. The brain runs on dual control, which means that it obeys both conscious and unconscious impulses. No one has credibly explained how this happens. Unconscious processes keep going without your instructions. You have no awareness of blood pressure, heart rate, digestion, the activity of your immune system, the balance of endocrine hormones, and so on. In sleep you lose awareness that you have a body altogether. When awake, you have thoughts without knowing how neurons operate. Indeed, in the absence of medical knowledge, there is no evidence you even have a brain.

It is normal for the brain to operate either under your instructions or on its own. The mystery behind this dual control deepens when we ask how the nervous system can tell the difference between conscious and unconscious activity. The nerves associated with breathing, for example, do their job automatically, with sensitivity to the situation you find yourself in. Breathing is a telltale barometer of fight, stress, tension, sexual desire, and fatigue—as well as external factors like the altitude, the amount of oxygen, pollutants, and allergens in the air, and so on. At the same time, you can personally intervene with an intention, such as deciding to take a deep breath. You can make yourself sigh or yawn, which ordinarily are involuntary. If you are about to sneeze and try to stop it, the two halves of the breathing mechanism, voluntary and involuntary, fight each other, and sometimes the sneeze wins no matter how hard you try to stop it.

I don't think it is credible to say that the brain is the one that decides whether or not to operate automatically. Such an explanation would make your brain more conscious than you are. It's as if a self-driving car not only obeyed its software but also controlled the driver. Putting a car in total command prevents the driver from making decisions. Or imagine you want to wave to a friend as she leaves on a train, but your brain on its own decides, "No, I want no part of goodbyes," and prevents you from raising your arm. That doesn't happen.

The reason this point isn't obvious to everyone is that the bodymind is so seamless that you yourself cannot always tell who is in control. All kinds of things—sudden anger, alarm, sexual desire, panic attacks, phobias, bad habits, addictions, compulsive behavior, obsessive thoughts, depression, anxiety— overtake a person as if they had a mind of their own. If you look at one of Shakespeare's most psychological sonnets, the issue of who is in charge plays a leading role.

Sonnet 129 is about sexual desire taking over and then letting go as soon as orgasm is reached. It begins

> *Th' expense of spirit in a waste of shame*
> *Is lust in action; and till action, lust*
> *Is perjured, murd'rous, bloody, full of blame,*
> *Savage, extreme, rude, cruel, not to trust,*
> *Enjoyed no sooner but despisèd straight,*
> *Past reason hunted; and, no sooner had*
> *Past reason hated as a swallowed bait*
> *On purpose laid to make the taker mad.*

In eight intense lines of poetry we grasp the extremity of the brain's dual control. A carnal impulse "beyond reason" takes charge. Lust is so powerful that Shakespeare describes it the way a savage dictator would be described in a totalitarian state (perjured, murd'rous, bloody, etc.). When lust has run its mindless course, there is the aftermath. Rationality returns, feeling ashamed and remorseful, and now lust looks in retrospect like bait laid in a trap to ensnare the person.

Why was Shakespeare so bent on tying sexual desire to shame? Perhaps it was a personal confession by a married man whose wife stayed behind in Stratford while Shakespeare was away in London for months at a time. Is a cheater confessing his dalliances publicly in a poem or just saying he was tempted? Shame could also reflect religious beliefs about sex as a sin, although the Elizabethans were a rowdy, loose-living bunch, especially in theater circles. Firebrand Puritan preachers tended to compare actors to cutpurses and whores. Seen in the light of voluntary and involuntary action, Sonnet 129 is more about the human condition than merely about sex taking over as if it had a mind of its own.

The mystery of who's in charge is underscored by an intriguing experiment with "Aha!" moments—moments of creative breakthrough in which a sudden insight occurs, seemingly out of the blue and often unexpectedly. Professor Joydeep Bhattacharya and his colleagues at the University of London asked a group of volunteers to solve a verbal puzzle in 60 to 90 seconds. If they didn't reach the solution by 90 seconds, they were given a hint. Only some subjects solved the puzzle, and their brainwaves, as measured by an EEG, predicted who would fall into each group.

Those who had a sudden insight about how to solve the puzzle showed a peak in high-frequency gamma waves. The brain location for these spikes was the right temporal lobe, which is responsible, among other things, for shifting mental gears. The spike in gamma waves occurred up to 8 seconds before the volunteer hit upon the answer. The researchers commented that this spike in gamma waves is the same activity that occurs in transformational thinking—the departure from everyday thinking into the experience of "Aha!" moments.

Speculating about where good ideas come from, one commentator on this experiment bravely located the source in a "network of cells exploring the adjacent possible connections that they can make in your mind." This conclusion only seems to be on the right track if you believe brain cells are capable of looking around, finding the right connections, and saying "Aha!" on their own before delivering an "Aha!" to your mind.

As a cyber engineer would explain how computer circuitry works, a gap is created between the machine's inner workings and what you experience on the monitor, where the screen shows words, photos, videos, and so on. When you watch a skydiver on YouTube, is the video happening in the circuitry of your computer or smartphone? Absolutely not. Only digital processing is happening in the circuitry of a computer. The video is happening in your awareness.

Likewise, the skydiver in the video isn't experiencing the exhilaration of free fall in his brain. The brain is organic circuitry processing various chemical ions and electrical signals. Skydiving happens in awareness. The brain's circuitry cannot have the experience any more than a computer parachuting out of an airplane can have the experience. Without a self, there is no experiencer. I'm not denigrating neuroscience—at the very least, an understanding of brain activity is needed to help find cures for brain-related diseases like epilepsy, Parkinson's, and Alzheimer's.

I only want to point out that human beings are not prisoners of circuitry and haven't been for thousands of years. Somewhere in our ancestry, an evolutionary leap occurred when *Homo sapiens* crossed over the gap from circuitry to awareness. The most sophisticated high-speed computer cannot make such a leap, for the simple reason that, like the brain, a computer has no experiences.

So who's in charge? The only viable answer is that no one is in charge. The bodymind is simply operating in one mode or the other, sometimes voluntary, sometimes automatic. There doesn't have to be anyone in charge, not even you. You are also part of the wholeness. If there has to be an answer, then we can say that consciousness is in charge of itself. There is nothing beyond consciousness that could be in charge. (I am stepping on religious toes, I know, but putting God in charge simply adds another level of consciousness. It doesn't go beyond consciousness, because you can't.)

A visualization might help. Think of the ocean. It can be stormy or calm. Warm and cold currents run through it. Beneath the surface lives the uncountable multiplicity of marine life. Each goes through its life cycle. Some are predators, some are prey. Who's in charge of the ocean? It can only be the ocean itself. It is a self-sustaining ecosystem. Similarly, consciousness is an ecosystem, responsible for everything that occurs in the bodymind.

TOTAL MEDITATION
Lesson 10: Unbounded

To a fish swimming in a coral reef there is no boundary to the ocean. As an ecosystem, the ocean created and sustained everything living inside it. Consciousness is the ultimate ecosystem. It truly has no boundaries, because, unlike a flying fish, which can leap out of the ocean to perceive (if it had a human brain) that there is a nonwatery ecosystem, no one can leap outside consciousness. Such a move is inconceivable.

We are connected to this unboundedness. Everything about consciousness in its totality is true about us, too. Meditation takes us closer and closer to the unbounded mind, which is the whole mind. When whole mind is experienced, limitations fall away. One realizes how unnecessary it is for the mind to impose so many boundaries on itself. Waking up makes you realize how pointless boundaries are, especially if you imagine they *must* exist.

On the journey to unbounded mind, the goal isn't reached at once—it is a process. But it helps to have a vision of the goal. Here are a few simple ways to connect with the unbounded for a moment or two.

- On a sunny, cloudless day, lie on your back so that your field of vision is filled with the clear blue sky. Let yourself relax into the sensation of this blueness, making it your primary sensation. Now look beyond the blue. There is no recipe for doing this, but just try. For a brief moment you can sense that the sky is the frontier, so to speak, of infinity.

- Close your eyes and imagine that you are a NASA probe traveling into deep space at tremendous speed, hundreds of miles a second. See the stars go by and distant galaxies coming closer. Accelerate faster and faster, then make the stars and galaxies disappear. Now there is only the black void, and there is no feeling of speed. You are suspended in unbounded space with no experience except its unboundedness.

- Listen to a piece of music that you love, and feel the sweet sensation of its beauty. Now stop the music but stay with the sweetness. The cause has disappeared, but the sweetness is there on its own. This is what unbounded bliss feels like—it needs no cause, existing all by itself.

If consciousness is in charge of itself, it can do anything and everything. But our personal experience is vastly different. We cannot do anything and everything. Often we feel that what we do is so feeble it hardly matters. This must change. Otherwise we are left with fantasies of power and possibility that do not turn into reality. Where is the total power of consciousness where it really counts, here and now? That's the question we will explore next.

4

The Stuckness Syndrome

Total meditation builds trust in consciousness to take care of your life, but if trust is the goal, what about the existence of evil? For centuries the human drama has portrayed good as contending with evil, thus undermining any theory that human beings are innately good. At the same time, the existence of evil has undermined the notion that God or the gods are totally benign. No God worth worshipping, an atheist will contend, would allow the horrors of war and genocide that have created deep wounds in our collective history, wounds that continue to this day.

Being stuck with the worst aspects of human behavior baffles us. There is ample evidence that at every level of our existence, from domestic abuse to civil war, from petty crime to mass murder, no good comes of evil. So why don't we give it up, for our own good? This question opens the door to the whole issue of stuckness—in other words, the persistence of negativity, which continues to have its way despite our best efforts and highest ideals. The roots of evil behavior exist in all of us. We alone are the source of war, crime, and violence. We may not act out the dark side of human nature. But if placed in a situation that is combustible enough, each of us has a breaking point, beyond which reason and goodness give way to irrational behavior fueled by anger, resentment, envy, revenge, intolerance, fear, and even the thrill of violence.

If it's true that we ourselves are the source of evil, then a practical solution to evil presents itself: Get unstuck. Experiences come and go; thoughts arise and quickly vanish; emotions last longer but also fade away. Anger and fear, the two most powerful negative emotions, won't fuel evil behavior if they rise and fall in the same rhythm as normal experiences. The flow of consciousness takes care of this until we interfere. We are the cause, and at the same time the victim, of what I'm calling the stuckness syndrome. This syndrome has always been the trap of evil—that the same mind indulges in the activity that hurts it the most.

If the goal is getting unstuck, you can set aside almost everything about theoretical evil. It is merely a theory that God and Satan are at war with each other, or that an invisible archetype of war has influence over us. Equally theoretical are all psychological explanations about the unconscious mind, where our worst impulses supposedly lie hidden, or where the "shadow" rules like a malicious dictator. Countless people believe in one or more of these concepts, but no theory has led to a solution. Let's set all explanations of evil aside, focusing instead on getting unstuck. The most that you can do is to free yourself from bad behavior. When anger and fear are passing shadows that disperse as quickly as they arose, you have accomplished something great. You have rid yourself of your share in the world's evil.

THE HABIT OF EVIL

The most basic thing about evil is that it has become a habit, something that gets repeated over and over until it becomes an automatic response. In that regard, evil is quite mundane. It has no special power to ensnare us but rather belongs in the pesky realm of other bad habits. Nearly all of us exhibit self-defeating, irrational behaviors on a daily basis, to the point that they become routine and habitual. Rather than doing everything we can to change for the better, we unconsciously cling to the very behaviors that block us at every turn. Sigmund Freud, the founder of psychoanalysis, investigated this kind of "pathological" self-defeating behavior in his 1901 book *The Psychopathology of Everyday Life*, a phrase that seems relevant to our look at evil in relation to stuckness.

The psychopathology of everyday life takes many forms. Evil, suffering, and woundedness overlap without the neatly separate categories we have created for them. Nevertheless, there are different kinds of experience that belong to everyday psychopathology, such as

Anxiety and depression

Compulsive behavior, obsessive thoughts

Self-judgment

Guilt

Shame

Damaged self-esteem

Lack of impulse control

Denial, or avoidance of what's wrong

*Repression, or pushing unwanted impulses out
    of sight*

No sensible person believes that any of these experiences are psychologically healthy. They create enormous distress and can become disabling at their worst. At the same time, none of these conditions will get better by hating them, blaming yourself, blaming others, or giving up on dealing with them. Feeling bad about yourself makes most of these problems worse, in fact, and good advice from others scarcely improves the situation.

What we label as evil isn't a single impulse or behavior. It is a composite of dark ingredients, none of them cosmically evil or even innately evil. The monstrous mass murderers in history magnify everyday impulses to disastrous degrees. Such everyday "dark" impulses include

Lashing out at others

Blaming someone else

Wanting to get back at the person who hurt you

Attacking first as a form of self-defense

Feeling powerless, which leads to revenge fantasies

Feeling hopeless, which leads to devil-may-care recklessness

Take an everyday situation like being bullied at school. You can't have a bully without having a victim. No one volunteers to be the victim, but children and adolescents have a limited repertoire of ways to cope. It hardly matters which role they play. Bullies and their victims both act out the same impulses. If you look back at the list just presented, both sides are blaming someone else, using attack and defense as their only options, feeling helpless or making someone else feel helpless, and so on. The monsters of history are no different; they simply enact their psychopathology ("disorder of the mind") on a grand scale because the millions of people they oppress would do the same in their place.

I don't mean that we are all potentially mass murderers, but rather that we get stuck in the same patterns of attack and defense, hurting or being hurt, seeking revenge and fantasizing about it, and so on. If your situation drives you to extremes of anger, resentment, powerlessness, and hopelessness, you are ripe for acting out what we label as evil or becoming its victim. Either role is a form of stuckness.

The way out is to develop more options in your behavior, which is done by becoming more conscious. Most people cope with a difficult situation through four basic behaviors:

Defending themselves

Fighting back

Putting up with the situation

Going into denial

If you are stuck in this limited range of behaviors, you will experience many situations, particularly in personal relationships and at work, that do not move ahead toward productive outcomes. In total meditation, the desirable outcome can be left for consciousness to resolve. This isn't a strategy many people find themselves using, although in an age of faith, leaving things to God was similar, the problem being that God was treated like a superhuman entity living in Heaven. This separation of the human and the divine stranded the devout in helpless passivity waiting for God's decision. Such a position wasn't viable, and human nature took over. An age of faith was not immune to violence and war, along with a plentiful display of the seven deadly sins.

Total consciousness isn't separate from you. It is your source and your true self. As awareness expands, you discover new resources that allow for a wider range of behaviors in difficult situations. There are times when a confrontation is hard to avoid, and turning it into a zero-sum game, in which someone has to lose for someone else to win, is rarely the right outcome. The seeds of hostility are sown, and festering resentment leads to the stuckness syndrome that fosters evil.

The alternative to a zero-sum game is usually compromise, which keeps the confrontation from escalating. In any difficult situation, whether the situation is a domestic rift or two countries that need to pull back from the brink of armed conflict, consciousness opens up the possibility for a peaceful outcome. You can give peace a chance through the following behaviors:

You actively seek a solution from people who can genuinely help.

You don't act on impulse but wait until you are centered.

You take responsibility for your feelings without lashing out or blaming someone else.

You trust that a solution is always possible.

You seek insight in meditation mode.

You leave stressful situations rather than endure them.

You don't become the cause of stress.

You respect others as your equal.

You value your own happiness and do not rationalize suffering as if it is a virtue.

There is nothing magical about this expanded range of behaviors—they have always been available. Some disastrous wars would have been avoided, and countless divorces averted, if these behaviors had been followed. It is testimony to how asleep people really are that so few of us know how to prevent conflicts by defusing the threats at an early stage.

Consciousness naturally unfolds these responses in the process of waking up. They arise in many people who have never heard of consciousness and do not practice meditation, simply in the course of becoming a mature adult. The process can be greatly sped up, however, by consciously favoring awakened behavior. The best way to live right now is to live as if you are awake.

We cannot expect expanded consciousness to work with school bullying. Children and adolescents are still in an immature and often confusing stage of psychological development. We don't hold them fully responsible for their behavior. If the wounds of childhood persist, however, the mature adult is just as wounded. Most of the psychopathology of everyday life comes from the damaged child within. (The popular notion of the inner child as somehow innocent and angelic ignores the psychological reality that alongside innocence every child harbors the negative impulses that eventually lead to stuckness.)

As you wake up, the psychopathology of everyday life becomes less troublesome, simply by your not needing to defend your ego personality. "I" is the problem and therefore can never be the solution. It doesn't take much self-awareness to see that the ego personality is insecure, selfish, demanding, and driven by impulses it struggles to control. What's harder to see is something much more basic. "I" is sticky. A housefly lands on a piece of paper and almost instantly leaves, unless it happens to land on flypaper. Likewise, experiences don't stick to us unless we are sticky. By the same token, you can't expect the ego to rid itself of its own stickiness. Whatever it takes to get unstuck, "I" isn't going to accomplish it.

TOTAL MEDITATION
Lesson 11: Habits

Total meditation replaces unconscious responses with conscious ones, and a very useful application of this shift centers on habits. Habits are a circular trap. The impulse behind a habit keeps repeating itself. When the impulse arises, most people struggle briefly, then give in. The habit has won, and it will win the next time it circles back unless you can break the circle.

The same model applies no matter what the habit happens to be. Overeating and worrying seem very different on the surface, but both are circular and both have roots in the unconscious (i.e., there is no obvious cause at the level of thinking, and trying to think your way out of the habit doesn't address the problem). The more awake you are, the easier it is to address the key element that keeps a habit going, which is repetition. Let's discuss this issue in terms of how the mind falls into repeated patterns, because this is the nub of the problem.

Consciousness accomplishes everything in silence, but the mind is full of noise. Much of this noise has little to do with useful or rational thought. When a tune gets stuck in your head, there's no reason it should keep repeating itself long after you've stopped enjoying it. The psychopathology of everyday life is rife with other examples that are less innocuous. Worriers constantly fret, unable to escape the vicious circle of fears that have no real possibility of coming true. At the clinical end of the spectrum, obsessive-compulsive disorder (OCD) condemns sufferers to persistent ritualized thoughts, such as counting the cracks in the sidewalk or adding up the numbers of license plates on cars.

What all of these conditions have in common is repetition. If we take away the clinical labels, it seems that everyone is subject to thoughts, memories, and impulses that return time and again. Old, outworn reminders of guilt and shame, humiliation and defeat, lost arguments and prickly grievances circle the mind as if on a toxic merry-go-round we're stuck on. Yet no one knows why the mind keeps returning over and over to thoughts that serve no good—these reminders are useless and unwelcome. They only serve to annoy and distress. Something you'd rather forget refuses to be forgotten.

Bad habits fit into the general scheme. Short of being diagnosed with OCD, few people seek professional help for repetitive thoughts, but at the same time we feel helpless to stop them. Consider these examples from daily life:

- You have vowed to quit eating between meals, but as you sit watching TV, the impulse to get up and grab a snack keeps coming back.
- You feel angry and irritated over something quite minor, such as being in line at the post

office and having somebody cut in front of you. You know you should be big enough to forget the incident, but you keep replaying it in your mind.

- You buy an everyday household item or piece of clothing, and when you get home, you see online that another vendor is having a half-price sale on the same item. The difference isn't significant, but you kick yourself for not checking things out more thoroughly.
- You are on vacation, looking forward to visiting a famous restaurant you've wanted to eat at for a long time. When you arrive, however, you are told that there is no reservation under your name, and unfortunately the restaurant is fully booked. After you get home from your vacation, you keep fretting over what might have gone wrong and how much you miss the great meal you will never have.

Despite the futility of repetition, the mind doesn't give up the behavior.

If you can learn to clear away repetitive thoughts, impulses, and mental habits, they will stop returning. You will gain a sense of being more in control, and the screen of your mind will be noise-free.

Here a deeper bit of understanding helps. These repetitive thoughts and impulses are fragments of the ego, and because "I" is sticky, so are its fragments. The ego personality is built entirely from past experiences, so naturally it cannot help but relive them, for one reason or another.

You don't have to figure out the reason. You are more than your ego. When it insists upon its viewpoint, you are free to offer another perspective, one that is more conscious. This is easily done, in any of the following ways:

- If an innocuous repetition like a tune running through your head is bothering you, pause and count back from 100 by threes. This simple focus brings the mind back to the present moment.
- If the thought is negative, reminding you of something you don't want to focus on, tell it, "I don't need you right now." This is a kind of negotiation with an ego fragment; you aren't fighting it or giving in either. Don't insist, but if the thought comes back, gently repeat, "I don't need you right now."
- If a repetitive thought is more insistent, such as the impulse to grab a snack, center yourself, take a few deep breaths, and sit in meditation mode.
- If the recurring thought is a worry, take pencil and paper and write down how you feel. Keep writing, letting the emotion go on as long as

it wants to. You might feel that you are scribbling gibberish, but worry is irrational. By letting it have its say, however childish or fretful, you defuse the emotional energy that feeds the worry.

- Whenever you feel that your mind is filled with noise, get out of thinking mode. For example, random mental noise is often associated with insomnia. The engine of the mind keeps running, even though you have no reason to keep thinking. Vagal breathing (page 26) is a very useful remedy here. Another way to get out of thinking mode is to visualize a patch of color in your mind's eye. Keep your attention on the color, and if thoughts distract you, easily return to the color.

None of these practices is intended to be effortful. In everyday life, repetitive thoughts eventually fade away. If you already know how to center yourself, you know the difference between being awake and being asleep. Habits and repetitive thoughts don't stick around when you are awake.

Yet it is still worth knowing that bothersome thoughts, memories, impulses, and habits are ego fragments. They stick with us because "I" is sticky. Be patient with getting unstuck. You have lived with 'I' for a long time, and every day in big and little ways you have adopted its viewpoint. Shifting into a different viewpoint requires you to return to meditation mode so often that it becomes the mind's new perspective. Every small experience of being in meditation mode—centered, at ease, and in balance—teaches the brain to remain there, and in time it will remain there permanently.

INTENTION AND RESISTANCE

Waking up gives us a more expanded perspective than the isolated ego personality. When you are awake, your awareness is unclouded by the things that affect "I" every day. Aligned with the infinite power of consciousness, desires are fulfilled easily, as if the path has been smoothed beforehand. Your intention reaches the desired goal in a straight line, as indicated in the following diagram.

Intention → Accomplishment

Having a conscious intention is how consciousness manages every successful outcome, without missteps along the way. With simple intentions—lifting your arm, driving a car, talking on the phone—the path to accomplishment is so automatic that we rarely think about it. Yet a disturbance along the way can block the whole process. I know a woman who was driving home from a restaurant at twilight. She was feeling relaxed after a glass of wine and a good meal. The country road she was on came to a T-stop, and after a pause she turned left. Carelessly she hadn't looked right, and an instant later an eighteen-wheeler smashed into her car. Only by a fraction of a second did she escape being killed.

Her narrow escape preyed on her mind. She let her husband take over all the driving from that day on; he had been in the back seat during the accident and had suffered very minor neck injuries. But the trauma of the accident left its mark on him. He lost his appetite for several months and lost twenty pounds. At the time of this writing, three years later, the woman has been psychologically unable to get behind the wheel of a car, even to drive one block on a nearly deserted street inside their condo community to get the mail. The same mind that learned to drive a car—a skill that some psychologists consider the most intricate one that most people master in everyday life—now feels paralyzed. It doesn't matter that the woman wants to drive. Her desire has been blocked.

There are countless ways that an unwanted outcome occurs, but a general pattern can be diagramed as follows:

Intention ➔ ⬅ Resistance

Every situation in which you are blocked, either by your own mind or by outside forces, fits this diagram. You want to do something (intention), but you meet with resistance. Pause for a moment and consider something about yourself you find very hard to change. For one person, it might be weight and body image; for another, lack of love; for yet another, a sense of frustration in relationship. Once you single out an example of stuckness, the following points are very likely to be true:

You've known about this problem for a while.

You have thought about it often.

You haven't made progress in solving it, or progress has been temporary.

No one has given you truly useful advice.

In your worst moments you feel helpless, hopeless, or both.

You keep repeating fixes that never worked in the first place.

In the end you simply put up with whatever has gone wrong.

This, in a nutshell, is how resistance gains the upper hand. Everyone is burdened with limitations that are created by running into resistance. "I" is part of this process, since the ego is shaped by disappointments in the past, all those times when things didn't go our way. The whole issue of stuckness depends upon a simple fact: Experiences come and go, but some leave a lasting impression. These impressions fall along a spectrum from very shallow to very deep. The first impression you get of another person can lead to lasting enmity or lifelong love, but usually it is somewhere in between. Your upbringing left a lasting impression on you even though you had no idea at the time that this was happening. Deep impressions get stuck; shallower ones vanish fairly quickly—the movie that made you cry might linger in the mind for a few hours or longer, but few movies remain in the mind much longer. There is no way to quantify the good and bad impressions created in a child's early experiences. We are marked by those experiences, without a doubt. At the same time, however, we compensate for the bad stuff and move ahead.

This pattern of response doesn't negate the fact that current solutions for getting unstuck are generally ineffective. Handing out information goes only so far, as evidenced by the fact that nearly a quarter of American adults continue to smoke more than fifty years after the link between smoking and lung cancer was definitively stated by the surgeon general. Nutrition labels on packaged foods have done next to zero in halting the country's obesity epidemic. Traditional psychotherapy has an equally poor track record with the most common forms of mental suffering. The multibillion-dollar market for antidepressants and tranquilizers grimly attests to failure, and these drugs merely improve symptoms in a given percentage of patients. The most advanced medical science has yet to find actual cures for depression and anxiety.

The essential problem is that the more we meet with resistance, the more likely we are to define ourselves in limiting ways. "I am depressed" or "I am anxious" turns into part of a person's self-image if the condition lasts long enough. Sometimes we blame ourselves for disappointing outcomes; at other times we blame external circumstances. Whatever we tell ourselves, however, we seem to inevitably begin to reduce our expectations when our dreams don't come true.

One of the chief causes of unhappiness is lowered expectations. From the viewpoint of consciousness, expectations should be unlimited. As we get unstuck, the prospects for higher expectations steadily improve. Yet, on a daily basis, the experience of meeting resistance needs to be resolved before your higher expectations can become real.

TOTAL MEDITATION

Lesson 12: Resistance

When life resists you, you have to do something. Imagine that you are traveling and you discover at the airport that your flight has been delayed. It's important to make your next connection, which is in doubt, depending on how long the present delay turns out to be. Life is resisting your plans, so what do you do? People usually pick from a menu of choices:

> You can sit there and stew.
> You can walk around or read a book to distract
>   yourself from the situation.
> You can complain at the check-in desk.
> You can negotiate to get on another flight.
> You can reschedule for the next day and go
>   home to relax.

There are other less likely options. If you are very rich, you might procure a private plane. Or, more realistically, if the flight is delayed because of the weather, you can opt to take a train instead. The range of responses is so wide that most of us rarely have any certainty about which one to choose. We wind up with inner confusion and conflict. A delayed flight is a simple problem. Responding to resistance can become much more complicated in other situations, such as in the workplace or in personal relationships.

Stuckness is the outcome when resistance wins. Moving forward is the outcome when your intention wins. You have control over the different outcomes.

When *resistance wins*, you have allowed yourself to fall into one or more of the following responses when you meet resistance:

You give in to anger, resentment, or fear.
You lose control of your options.
You fall back on old responses that are unlikely to work.
You vacillate out of doubt.
You hunt for who to blame.
You give up because "they" are too strong to fight against.
You become a victim.
You try to push or bully your way through the obstacle.
You walk away without a solution.
You ask someone else to solve the problem for you.

The above list is the anatomy of frustration. None of the responses actually get you out of stuckness, even when your tactics may win in the short run. The next time you meet with resistance, you will again plunge into inner confusion and conflict, flailing around to get past the resistance. There are people who stick with only one response. They always bully, for example, or always give in and do nothing. But these people are stuck—the very problem we're trying to solve.

In contrast, when *you win* in the face of resistance, you have made use of one or more of the following responses when you meet resistance:

You don't give in to anger, resentment, or fear.
You can clearly see your possible options.
You don't fall back on old responses that are unlikely to work.
You don't make any decisions when in doubt.
You blame no one, including yourself.
You don't fight with yourself or others.
You trust in a good outcome.
You don't push or bully your way through the obstacle.
You remain open to unexpected solutions.

As you can see, quite a few factors are involved when you meet resistance in your life, but most people do not see the complexity of things as they really are. If they meet with opposition, they react with the same reflex they always use. Marital arguments repeat the same pattern year after year, for example. But it would be futile to try to address every item on the list of things that conspire when resistance wins.

The bottom line is more clear-cut: Either resistance wins or you win. This isn't oversimplification. It goes back to the premise that when we are in balance, the body-mind is aligned with total consciousness. Only total consciousness can control all the diverse elements that are in play. This holds true in the life of a cell and is just as true in our daily life

5

Getting Unstuck

Getting unstuck takes place entirely in consciousness, because that is the location of all experiences. Total meditation takes advantage of this fact in a way that nothing else can. If you cannot forget something or forgive someone in your past, there is no physical remedy. Consciousness alone can alter consciousness. Memory-erasing drugs don't exist, and if they did, it's hard to see how a drug could target one bad memory while leaving the good ones intact.

In English, the word *impression* evokes images of physical marks, like the impression of a fingerprint left at a crime scene or footprints in the snow. But in reality consciousness imprints itself. Seeking for answers in the memory centers of the brain isn't fruitful. You need a brain in order to remember things, the way you need a television to turn electronic signals into pictures on a screen. If you drop the television from a two-story window, there will be no more pictures, yet the signals are unaffected.

Similarly, the brain makes thoughts, images, and memories

from signals that originate in consciousness. If you suffer a concussion, the trauma to the brain can create temporary amnesia, and obviously permanent memory loss is one of the most dreaded aspects of Alzheimer's disease. Brain injuries and dementia indicate that memory has been damaged, but this says little about normal memory. In fact, normal memory remains almost entirely a mystery. It is true that memory research has advanced in recent decades beyond what medical school students used to be taught—namely, that for all we knew about memory, the head might as well be filled with sawdust. Today, researchers can create false memories in people and erase memories in laboratory animals. We are already good at doing both on our own, however.

The acclaimed English neurologist Oliver Sacks was seven in the autumn of 1940 when the London Blitz began. His family lived in the zone where German airplanes dropped incendiary bombs. These were bombs filled not with explosives, but with highly combustible chemicals such as magnesium, phosphorus, or flammable petroleum (napalm). Their purpose was to create widespread fires and spread terror. Sacks remembers his father running into the backyard with buckets of water after an incendiary bomb fell, only to discover that when water is poured on a magnesium or phosphorus fire, the flames suddenly expand, making the fire worse.

Only decades later, when Sacks came to write about memory, did he find out from his older brother that none of these vivid memories was true. Like all very young children, Sacks was sent to the countryside during the Blitz. He wasn't present when incendiary bombs fell in the backyard. Those memories belonged to his older brother, who had been present, and Sacks had absorbed them from stories he had been told. In this case, the real memory, of being away from home in the country, was erased, and a false memory replaced it.

At bottom, since we have no idea how thoughts are created in the first place, our understanding of how they are remembered or forgotten lies shrouded in darkness. It would be more helpful if we had an English equivalent for the Sanskrit term *samskara*, which refers to the impressions in consciousness that shape our actions. Samskaras can be good, such as musical or artistic talent, or undesirable, like a tendency toward violence.

Because a samskara is laid down in the past, memory comes into play, but no one knows why one memory makes an indelible impression while another doesn't. One clue is emotion. If a strong emotion is associated with an experience, the resulting memory is also likely to be stronger and more vivid. That's why you probably remember your first kiss, but not the color of your neighbor's car that same year. Yet this knowledge is quite basic. It is fairly obvious that strong emotions make memories more indelible than neutral experiences that do not elicit strong feelings. Around the world, a whole generation remembers hearing the news that President Kennedy had been shot. It became the kind of memory in which millions of people can still see where they were when the shocking news arrived. Smaller, more personal memories are much more elusive.

Researchers into memory are far from knowing why memory is selective, imperfect, and personal. It isn't even known how much of the past anyone remembers. There are a hand-ful of exceptional people who can recall every moment of the past, including the pattern on the wallpaper of their bedroom when they were five, the songs they heard, and the TV shows they watched on any specific date, or what the score was in the third inning of the World Series—in short, their recollection is flawless.

This condition, known as superior autobiographical mem-ory, affects a minuscule number of people, and no one knows whether the average person has their entire past stored away or not. Perhaps the problem isn't memory, but recall. We need to be humble enough in the modern West to concede that genetics offers no better explanation than simple everyday experience. When a child resembles their parents in some way, the saying "It runs in the family" is nearly as accurate as identifying a specific gene. In both cases, mere probability is being expressed, and sometimes not even that. Your height, for example, is influenced by more than twenty separate genes, along with diet and other factors in your childhood.

Innate tendencies like talent and genius defy genes entirely. On YouTube, for example, you can see a seven-year-old child, Himari Yoshimura of Japan, playing the Paganini Violin Con-certo No. 1. The piece requires dazzling virtuosity, and the fact that Yoshimura won first prize at a prestigious violin competi-tion in 2019, at an age when some children are still learning to tie their shoes, utterly overturns current knowledge about the capacity of the early development of the brain.

Whether we have the right name for imprinted memories,

shared family traits, innate tendencies, genius, prodigious talent, or everyday experiences that prove to be sticky, the question is, How do we get past these samskaras when they limit us? It takes the intervention of consciousness. Here we're talking about psychological limitations, since physical samskaras such as an inherited disorder or birth defect are another matter. Let me illustrate what is meant by a psychological limitation rooted in the past.

A child struggling in school needs support and help from teachers and parents. If it isn't forthcoming, a small voice inside the child begins to say, "No one is ever going to help you." Worse still, if the child is made to feel stupid or damaged, the small voice starts saying, "You aren't good enough."

Recently, I met a middle-aged man—let's call him Randy—who was a skilled software programmer, but he had so little self-confidence that he found it very hard to find or hold a job. When we spoke, he brought up a traumatic experience from his childhood. In first and second grades, he couldn't absorb even simple lessons the teacher was imparting, which caused him to shrink inside himself and rarely speak. The school determined that he had learning disabilities, and his parents agreed to have him put in a special needs class. He continued to perform poorly there, and being around children who had been dumped into the class because of behavioral problems frightened him.

Two years passed this way, at which point his parents noticed for the first time that Randy had a hard time catching a ball. An eye examination revealed that he was extremely nearsighted. It turned out that Randy had a higher-than-average IQ but had failed in school because he couldn't see the blackboard. It was as simple as that. He then returned to the normal school track, where he performed well now that he could see, but he was scarred by being misunderstood, judged, and considered inferior for two long years.

As an adult, early in his twenties, Randy began to meditate, and his traumatic experience began to lose its sting in two ways. He found he didn't identify with it any longer, and when the old hurtful memories happened to resurface, they no longer made him feel so bad, indications that he was getting free of the past in general. The process of freeing oneself from the imprint of samskaras can happen naturally as the ego, which has deep roots in the past, gives way to a more expanded sense of self—in Randy's case, through meditation.

I was reminded of a saying I first heard as a child in India: Samskaras are first written in stone, then in sand, then in water, and finally in air. The saying poetically expresses how consciousness lessens the effect of impressions from the past. But what is the process, as expressed in practical terms? To answer this question, we need to look more closely at how past experiences get stuck in the first place.

TOTAL MEDITATION
Lesson 13: Stickiness

Sticky is a useful term for experiences that leave a deep impression, because they stick around and at the same time stick like glue. This image is easily understood, but it is just an image. No one can predict in advance which experience will stick and which will simply slide by without leaving an impression. Our concern is in the present, however. Getting unstuck happens here and now. Explanations from the past are intriguing but not really relevant. For example, memory studies have shown that when you seize on the memory of something traumatic in the past, such as being a three-year-old who panics in the supermarket because you can't see your mother, the memory is untrustworthy. Often it conflates several experiences of panic that are not recalled. Moreover, the details of the memory are more dreamlike than photographic. You might have been lost in a hardware store or a parking lot.

For practical purposes, stickiness can be approached through two of its aspects: belief and emotions. Experiences stick to us when we believe that they add something true to our personal story, and they will be even stickier if a strong emotional charge lingers around them. Let's look at belief first. Pause for a moment and think of a personal quality you believe is true about yourself, expressed as "I am _____." Fill in the blank with one positive word like *likable, attractive,* or *intelligent,* although there is usually stronger belief attached to negative words like *antisocial, dumb, clumsy,* and *unattractive.*

Whatever quality you picked didn't come out of the blue. It was embedded as a belief under conditions that made it stick. Rooted beliefs generally feature the following four elements:

We believe the first person who told us something.
We believe things that are repeated often.
We believe the people we trust.
We didn't hear a contrary belief.

It would be typical, if you believe you are either attractive or unattractive, that the first person who told you so was one of your parents. With that seed implanted, you heard the same thing said over and over or else went through repeated experiences that reinforced it. You trusted your parents as a small child and believed what they told you. Finally, no one came along to contradict your belief.

Personal things our parents told us, known as normative statements, are especially potent. "You are lazy," "You aren't as pretty as other girls," or "You will never amount to much" are taken to be actual facts by young children. But they are infused with subjective values, or norms. Saying "You got an A in arithmetic" lacks subjective impact compared with a normative statement like "You are so smart, you got an A in arithmetic." The latter statement is much more likely to be sticky.

The sticky things you were told about yourself become embedded as samskaras. The impression can be deep or shallow as it gets blended into the cumulative story of your whole life. The influence of a sticky experience is entirely personal. Being told that you aren't as pretty as other girls could lead to a range of reactions. You might grow up envying women you think of as prettier than you; you might think beautiful equals dumb; you could neglect your personal appearance or become fixated on cosmetics—any reaction is possible.

It is part of waking up to see the difference between reality and illusion. Consciousness works on everything in your life, but you can also focus on beliefs you have adopted unconsciously. Becoming conscious about sticky beliefs involves a kind of dissection—you look at the four elements behind strong beliefs, asking:

Who first told me this?
Was it repeated a lot?
Why did I trust the person who told me?
Is there reason to believe the opposite?

In other words, you turn around the experiences that made your belief sticky, and by turning them around, the belief becomes less and less sticky. If your mother told you that you aren't pretty or your father that you are lazy, why should you automatically trust them? It doesn't matter how often you heard their opinion. Now that you are an adult, you can separate opinion from fact. Think of experiences that indicated how attractive you are in other people's eyes or how diligently you applied yourself to a task.

The point is to get in touch with the damaged child inside you rather than allowing it to continue to dictate what you believe. The most important areas to concentrate on are your deepest personal beliefs, known as core beliefs. Core beliefs lock in your perspective on some crucial questions:

Is life fair?
Can other people be trusted?
Is there a higher power in the universe?
Does good triumph over evil?
Should I expect the best or prepare for the worst?
Should my attitude be relaxed or vigilant?
Am I safe?
Am I loved, cared for, and supported by others, or can I count only on myself?
Am I good enough and kind enough?

You certainly have some belief one way or another about all of these things, even though some questions will be more important to you than others. There are no factual answers to guide you. "I am safe" or "I am lovable" are subjective evaluations. They are rooted in how the ego personality got constructed. As an adult, you can see that your core beliefs have a lot to do with how you were raised. Either your parents' subjective opinions turned into your subjective opinions, or the contrary: you believe the opposite of what they believed. In this way, "I" is constructed from a value system that is essentially baseless and secondhand.

When you see how creaky even your most cherished beliefs actually are, you have seen reality. Now you are free to create your own core beliefs, which is what mature adults do. They have their own personal values. They make judgments based on actual facts and direct experience. They are not unduly influenced by secondhand opinions. These are good developments, psychologically speaking, but at bottom all beliefs are illusory. They lead to blanket responses—like thinking that life is unfair or other people cannot be trusted—that are inherently unreliable. Life changes all the time. It is never fair or unfair as a rule, not even as a rule of thumb. Likewise, the next person you meet might be totally trustworthy or a slippery liar.

The solution is to go beyond all beliefs. This is the goal in total meditation. By living in the present without the baggage of old beliefs, you are awake to the situation at hand. The point of dissecting your core beliefs is to bid them farewell. An unhealthy belief is the fossil of unreliable thoughts in your past. There is no need to hold on to them.

The second aspect of stickiness is that it is emotional. Emotions are stickier than facts. If an aggressive dog terrified you as a small child, the fact that most dogs are harmless and friendly isn't likely to change your attitude toward them. Being teased for stuttering is hurtful even though your parents might tell you that the majority of stutterers outgrow the problem after childhood.

Earlier I mentioned that a tiny number of people, perhaps two dozen in the world, have the ability to remember every event in their past with photographic accuracy. However, this condition, superior autobiographical memory, isn't as neutral as a photograph—the emotions associated with the memory return at the same time. As one woman ruefully observed, thanks to her perfect memory, she could recall all the times her mother told her she was fat.

The stickiest part of a memory is its emotional charge, which some psychologists have termed our emotional debt from the past. We stubbornly hold on to old resentments, grievances, fears, and wounded feelings. When positive and negative electrical charges build up in the clouds, we see the explosive discharge of lightning and thunder. In humans, the same occurs when someone says "That's the last straw!" and proceeds to release built-up anger.

The trick is to discharge emotional energy without a sudden explosion. There are ways to release old anger, fear, and resentment without allowing them to build up. Or if you are already holding on to these stored-up feelings, the same techniques are just as useful. The difference is that the longer you have been holding on to emotions, the longer it takes to release them.

HOW TO DISCHARGE STICKY EMOTIONS

The following techniques for discharging sticky emotions are easy and natural. Emotions by their very nature rise and fall, and most of the time a cooling-off period suffices to return you to a settled state. But sticky emotions don't fade away on their own. They ask you to assist by discharging them through various practices.

TECHNIQUE #1: If you feel an uncomfortable emotion that persists, center yourself and take slow, deep breaths until you feel the emotional charge start to lessen.

TECHNIQUE #2: If you recognize an emotion that has been around a long time, notice its return, then say: "This is how it once was. I am not in the same place now. Go away."

TECHNIQUE #3: With a particularly stubborn

emotion, sit quietly with eyes closed and let yourself feel the emotion—do this lightly, not sinking deeply. Take a deep breath and exhale slowly, releasing the emotional energy from your body. It might help to see your breath as a white light carrying the toxic feeling out of you.

TECHNIQUE #4: If you feel no specific emotion, but rather a general mood of being down, blue, or out of sorts, sit quietly with your attention placed in the region of your heart. Visualize a small white light there, and let it expand. Observe the white light as it expands to fill your whole chest. Now expand it up into your throat, then your head, and up out of the crown of your head.

Take a few minutes to carry this technique through until it feels complete. Now return to your heart and expand the white light again until it fills your chest. Now see it expand downward, filling your abdomen, extending down to your legs, and finally out through the soles of your feet into the earth.

These four techniques can be applied separately or one after the other. But it is important to be patient. Once you use a technique, it will take time for your whole emotional system to adapt to the discharge. You might not immediately feel better. But the intention to discharge sticky emotions is powerful, and the message gets through to every cell and every corner of your awareness.

Remember, too, that emotions want to discharge. This is in their nature. So they will leave you if you create a path for them to follow. It is your choice whether to let them discharge or to harbor reasons to hold on to them. These reasons are ego based. "I" feels justified in holding grudges, never ignoring a slight, nursing grievances, and fantasizing about revenge. Your true self has no such agenda. If you are sensitive, the next time you go off on an emotional tangent, or see someone else going off on one, you will notice that the ego derives a kind of self-righteous pleasure from displaying its stored anger.

But this pleasure is shortsighted. In the long run, sticky emotions keep you tied to the ego and deprive you of the awakened life. Paying some attention to discharging old emotions and sincerely wanting them to go are signs that you are awakening. If it could, "I" would hold on to toxic emotions forever, believing mistakenly that they are somehow worth hoarding. They aren't.

6

Self-Empowerment

Total meditation expands your awareness, and with that expansion comes personal power. Power based on awareness is not only possible but also automatic, and therein lies a secret. The typical image of a powerful person is attached to social markers like money, status, and the ability to dictate to others. And, unfortunately, as we've seen throughout history, those few who achieve great power tend to lord it over those who have less power or who feel powerless.

The actual source of power is mysterious, and when the richest and most prominent public figures are being candid, they are often baffled by their rise to the top. Most will say that luck played a big part—they were in the right place at the right time. Leaving good fortune aside, the path to self-empowerment needs to be clarified and made practical.

You might be well satisfied with your life choices up to now, an indication that things are going well for you. Most people, however, look upon their life choices as a mixture of good and bad. Whatever your attitude, no amount of success so far is the same as living from a starting point of infinite possibilities. In total meditation, you reframe your expectations by living closer and closer to your source of total consciousness. Then self-empowerment starts to take care of itself. That is, you naturally align with the level of consciousness that organizes the right outcome for any situation or challenge. If your desires are aligned with positive goals, the whole issue of empowerment has been solved.

TOTAL MEDITATION
Lesson 14: Least Effort

Whether to say yes or no is probably the most basic choice people make every day. The decision is made over and over, and people who are in the habit of saying no much of the time don't make life easy. Saying yes all the time also has its own share of problems. We wind up saying yes or no basically by repeating a choice we've made many times in the past. Acting out of habit is arbitrary. Parents get exasperated when a child keeps rejecting any new food with "I don't like it," to which the frustrated answer is "You haven't even tasted it yet." When we reject the new and unknown as adults, we are basically reverting to that childish habit of saying no without actually using any thought.

The issue can be reframed in terms of resistance. If you met with no resistance in your life, there would be much less reason to say no. Where does resistance come from? When other people resist us, the urge is to become annoyed and to push back. But the hidden resistance that exists inside us is something we need to pay great attention to. No one would argue with the following points:

- Other people are more accepting if you don't resist them.
- Getting what you want often involves giving someone else what they want.

- Cooperation achieves more results than not cooperating.
- You can't stop someone else from reacting to you the way they want to react.
- It is easy to say no to things that are new and unknown.

Everyone has to deal with life along these lines, but when you understand the nature of consciousness, each item on the list changes. Because consciousness is total, *it never resists itself*. The ocean can get stormy, but no matter how turbulent the waves, it isn't resisting itself. It has simply gone into a new mode, stormy instead of calm. Consciousness gives rise to all kinds of storms in human behavior. We don't have to tick off the violence, disharmony, controversies, and conflicts that have bedeviled history. Everyday life faces you with the opportunity to struggle or give in, to join in an argument or stand aside. There is no pattern of behavior that suits all situations. Society exults over victory in war and in the next breath venerates a pacifist like Gandhi.

These contrary impulses will persist and remain at war without a deeper vision. In its own nature, consciousness is orderly and organized. It unfolds its power along the line of least effort. We see this in the perfect organization of a cell, which wastes not a molecule of oxygen and nutrients. Nature as a whole operates through laws of motion, heat, gravity, and so on that have one thing in common: they take the shortest path from A to B, because it requires the least effort. The falling apple that, according to legend, gave Isaac Newton his "Aha!" moment about gravity didn't fall in a zigzag or take a brief detour to fall upward. Straight lines are the norm in Nature as long as there are no obstacles in the way.

Least effort isn't just efficient. It is the most powerful way to reach any goal. It has the least friction and gets around obstacles as swiftly as possible. If you translate this into everyday life, self-empowerment then looks very different. You can adjust every choice to be in line with least effort, as follows:

- Don't immediately push back or say no without first relaxing, centering yourself, and letting your deeper awareness respond. If given a chance, deeper awareness prefers to bring about the right result with the least effort. Don't act impulsively.
- When faced with a stressful situation, consciously ask yourself if the path of least resistance is open to you. If so, take it.
- Learn to allow and let go more often instead of insisting and trying to take control.
- Favor consensus and cooperation.
- Don't bully, coerce, or fall back on "Because I said so, that's why."

- Seek as much outside input as you can from people who are at least as aware as you are.
- Avoid people who typically do the opposite of everything mentioned above.

It's important to note that least effort is not acquiescence or mental laziness. The main reason we haven't already adopted least effort as a path to consciousness and self-empowerment comes down to social conditioning. A whole mythology surrounds the rewards of never giving up, fighting back, winning at all costs, and vanquishing the enemy. In the beginning, you might be tempted by this mythology, but consciousness shows a better way.

Least effort is applicable here and now, but you need to remember that any power derived from consciousness gets stronger the deeper your awareness is. As you meditate over time and practice least effort more and more, you will get closer to the source of pure awareness. And your choices will become increasingly successful because you have the orderliness and organizing power of consciousness supporting you.

When you change your starting point, the whole picture of self-empowerment changes. Imagine that you are about to enter a room where you will be challenged by someone in authority, say an IRS tax agent, a lawyer, or your boss. You don't know how this encounter will turn out. How does this prospect make you feel? Some people will stand up for themselves, their work, and their opinions vigorously, while others are meek, nervous, or easily intimidated.

You know yourself well enough to realize how you'd probably react. Yet your self-knowledge in this case is actually about limitation. On the surface the person with the strongest ego might look superior to someone who is quiet and self-effacing. Yet there is no predicting which one will make the right choices. Indeed, we often resort to secondhand sources of power, trying to look strong, successful, and in control, while deep down we are baffled by how life works.

We remain baffled because we are disconnected from the source of power. The difference between being connected and disconnected is clear-cut once you understand how consciousness works. Whenever you have to make a decision, the process isn't as rational as people suppose.

Pause for a moment and reflect on the last important decision you made. It can be anything. Buying a new house or changing jobs happens rarely, but you may have decided to speak up on an issue, offer advice to a friend or family member, make a presentation at work, or buy something expensive that needed consideration.

In the midst of your decision making, qualities of consciousness came into play. You may have found yourself in one of the following positions:

You were confident in yourself and certain that you'd make the right choice. You had a definite purpose in mind. You were in control. You didn't have second thoughts.

Or

You were tentative and doubtful. You vacillated one way or another. You weren't sure the outcome would be what you wanted. You were prone to worry and second thoughts.

It is these qualities of awareness that indicate how empowered you felt when you made your last important decision. Rational considerations entered in, certainly, but they were only part of the mix. If you were feeling really indecisive, you probably made your ultimate choice on impulse. Who is immune to buyer's remorse?

If you want to be confident instead of doubtful, how do you go about it? Most often people choose to disguise their doubts and put up a more confident front than what they actually feel. You fall back on protecting your ego image rather than finding a level of consciousness where confidence, direction, certainty, purpose, meaning, control, and successful outcomes are the norm. Ego won't get you there. This is why going beyond ego is a major part of total meditation.

The problem is that ego plays such a huge part in our decision making that it is hard to step off it. When you read the claim I just made that there is a level of consciousness where successful outcomes are the norm, how did you react? If you experienced doubt or skepticism, you were responding from ego. I don't mean egotism, which is exaggerated ego. In daily life, whether you are self-centered or modest, ego is your individual viewpoint. It encompasses your experiences and memories, habits and beliefs, in other words, the whole story you have been living up to this moment.

Stepping off ego is so foreign that most people really have no conception of what this means. That's totally understandable. Pure consciousness has no identity, no "I" to defend. It has no ties to memories, habits, and old conditioning, because only the present moment is its focus. As an experience, pure consciousness is a blank from the ego's standpoint. The ego registers an experience chiefly through desire and self-interest. "I want X" and "I don't want X" are prime considerations. "I like how this feels" and "I don't like how this feels" also play an important part, as does "Is this good or bad for me?"

When desire and self-interest are missing, the ego feels devoid of experience. The experience of pure consciousness rests upon simply being here, observing, allowing, and acting in the right way without second thoughts or self-interest. Standing back turns experience upside down. Instead of the mind being constantly active and restless—with the occasional moment of quiet, peace, and ease—you are always at peace and easy, with occasional moments in which something arises to say, think, or do.

The contrast is so stark that many people reject the state of quiet ease their mind naturally wants to be in. To them, inner calm feels like "nothing is going on," so they seek an immediate source of activity and distraction. Have you ever found yourself feeling a bit at loose ends or jittery? Suddenly you jump up to get a snack, check your texts, or channel-surf, generally without thinking or really needing to do any of these things. Impulsive behavior arises as a rejection of simply being here. The ego senses its own restlessness in a place of genuine quiet and ease, and "nothing is going on" becomes the trigger for pointless mental activity.

No one can be expected overnight to step off the plane of ego onto the plane of infinite possibilities—such a leap is more or less inconceivable. But we can fall back on the basic truth that consciousness is everywhere, participating in everything. It participates in how we lead our life, thus offering us a midway point that is totally human and yet far more expanded than the ego. This midway point is where you, the individual, encounter the organizing power of consciousness, the power that oversees the entire bodymind. From here, all the benefits of the awakened life are available.

THE HUMAN MATRIX

If we are told that total consciousness is supporting us in everything we do, we have the right to ask, "What is it doing for me today?" This is not a selfish or a presumptuous question. If you examine your life closely, it turns out that consciousness is doing not just a lot for you every day—it is doing everything. So far, I've used comparisons between less power and more power, but in reality you don't have to compare yourself to anyone else. Being total, consciousness cannot give you less power or more power. It offers everything to everyone. It's like being alive. When you are alive, you are just alive—it isn't a matter of half alive or one-tenth alive. Life exists as one thing. Microbes have this one thing, and so do whales, mole rats, iguanas, and you.

As human beings, we are embedded in a network that organizes, governs, and manages existence down to the level of the smallest thought as well as the smallest subatomic particle. I call this network the *human matrix*. This is the midway point between pure consciousness and the ego. In the human matrix, consciousness has constructed a setup tailored to our lives. There is a different matrix for other creatures. A sperm whale whose entire bodymind is set up to dive thousands of feet under the sea to locate and eat giant squid lives in a matrix, just as we do. We cannot claim that a sperm whale's matrix is simpler or more primitive than ours.

When consciousness creates a matrix, no one can have complete knowledge of how it is done. First of all, the process is invisible. Second, it leaves very few footprints behind. Chemical reactions inside a cell are perfectly organized, but they vanish after a few thousandths of a second. A thought delivers a meaningful message, but then it disappears without a trace. The human matrix is dynamic, changing all the time, something that works tremendously to your advantage. You are surrounded by the total power of consciousness working for you automatically, and it has complete knowledge about what you need.

Every time you have a new desire or intention, the whole matrix reacts. I have spent a great deal of time exploring the connection between quantum physics and consciousness. I can trace my fascination with this back to a quote from the eminent English physicist Sir Arthur Eddington, who said, "When the electron vibrates, the universe shakes." The same is true of the human matrix. Every desire you have, no matter how small, vibrates through consciousness and creates a change in its living structure.

We cannot see the organizing power that lies behind everything we think, say, and do. We cannot see intelligence on a brain scan, either, but it exists. No measuring device can quantify how much love you feel, but everyone who has fallen in love feels its enormous power. The human matrix has been in place for hundreds of thousands of years, evolving with every advance made by *Homo sapiens*. The higher brain of our remote Stone Age ancestors was organized so that mathematics, literature, and science were already being anticipated thousands of years before their first glimmering signs appeared. Our brain is constructed from DNA that is 85 percent the same as that of a mouse, 98 percent the same as that of a gorilla, and 99 percent the same as that of a chimpanzee, our nearest genetic relation.

But in that tiny sliver of a difference, the human matrix has been constructed. No one knows how that is possible, because relying on DNA to tell the story is misleading and inadequate.

Homo sapiens has been around for no more than 200,000 years; chimpanzees first appeared 18 million years ago. Chimps have higher brains, too, but the chimp matrix has close to zero potential for mathematics, literature, and science. They occupy a matrix that is complete for them, and if evolution occurs, it must be happening very, very slowly. We can presume, although we will never know for certain, that ancestral chimpanzees probably behaved very much like present-day examples.

The human matrix has evolved at lightning speed by comparison. If Stone Age humans had the potential for mathematics, literature, and science, they didn't know it, just as a two-year-old has no idea it has the potential to read. When you learned to read, you were playing evolutionary catch-up. Your consciousness unfolded its potential step-by-step. Yet these steps came from the past. Being able to speak, read, and think rationally is an inheritance—we acquire it automatically, simply by being born.

Once you reached maturity, however, you became the point person for evolution in the present. Standing on the shoulders of our ancestors, you can push the human matrix—your portion of it, anyway—wherever you desire. So where are you going next? No road map exists—how could it, with seven billion people constantly making choices every minute? If you stand back, however, there are links that unite human beings across all of recorded history. These links are our invisible potential, and they make us a unique species of consciousness. We can direct our own evolutionary path.

If you pause for a moment and look at your hand, you can

observe directly how consciousness works. The human hand has twenty-seven bones, the same number as in the hand of a chimpanzee. The main difference is that when you relax your hand, your thumb rests against the palm—this is the famous opposable thumb that evolutionists talk about. Chimps and other higher primates also have an opposable thumb, which they use to peel bananas, to groom each other, and to fashion a primitive tool from a twig that they use to poke for grubs in a tree.

What makes the opposable thumb an evolutionary miracle in humans cannot be seen in our bones. The miracle occurred in consciousness and is therefore invisible. The opposable thumb made it possible for humans to do fine detail work, as when an artist makes an engraving by using a stylus to scratch fine lines onto a copper plate. There is such an engraving, which Rembrandt etched of himself as a young man. His delicately rendered frowzy hair encircles his head like a tangled halo. The etching would be remarkable enough without knowing that the original is only about two inches across. (You can see it online by googling "Rembrandt self-portrait etching." It's the one with him looking over his left shoulder.) As adroit as chimps are, they can't do what Rembrandt did or, for that matter, what a street artist with a flourish of spray paint can do on a brick wall in a New York alley.

The fineness of detail required to cut a diamond, paint a cameo portrait, or make Venetian lace requires an opposable thumb, but it is just a tool, a tool useful to consciousness. Without consciousness, the tool is useless, or of limited use in the primate family.

When you consider every department of human life, you can see how unique the human matrix is, and how totally it embraces us.

THE HUMAN MATRIX

Everything consciousness has given us

Biology (organizing and running the body)

Survival instincts (fight or flight)

Perception (the five senses)

Psychology (personality, emotions, moods, etc.)

Rational thought

Social bonds, personal relationships

Language

Creativity

Curiosity, discovery, invention

Self-awareness

There are two amazing things about this list. First is its complexity. No other living creature uses consciousness with such diversity. Second is its unity. Consciousness is doing everything all at once. These two features—*diversity* and *unity*—combined define *totality*. It would be better if we didn't have to use abstract terms like *totality*, but there's a reason. Wholeness isn't an experience. In the human matrix, everything is being coordinated at the same time, but experiences occur singly in separation.

To get around this obstacle, here's an exercise that demonstrates what totality is doing out of sight.

Read the following sentence, which I picked at random, and as you do, count the number of times the letter *e* appears while at the same time trying to understand what the words mean.

> *There are, by best estimate, although no one knows for sure, somewhere between 100,000 and a million types of proteins in our bodies.*

It's obvious, I think, that your mind resists doing two things at once—it wants you to either read the sentence for meaning or count the number of times the letter *e* appears. Such is the limitation of linear experience. Yet at every moment of your life, the totality of consciousness has no difficulty managing everything I listed on page 159, from bodily processes to emotions, rational thought, and so on—the entirety of the human matrix. You live within the human matrix at the pinnacle of what consciousness is able to achieve on Earth. This realization radically redefines who you are.

If you understand what totality is, normal expectations become ridiculously inadequate to describe the power that exists inside and outside you. In fact there is no inside and outside. The totality of consciousness governs creation without regard for boundaries. This invisible structure, the human matrix, expands the meaning of total meditation. We must regard meditation as all-embracing, affecting everything in the human matrix. Here again the analogy of the ocean helps. One of the most surprising—and distressing—aspects of climate change is how rapidly the world's oceans have been affected by small changes. Alarming news reports tell us that as of 2019, more than a third of the coral reefs on the globe had suffered serious damage or died.

No one suspected that warming the seas by a few degrees Celsius could have such drastic effects. The Great Barrier Reef off the east coast of Australia has suffered from the sudden proliferation of a coral-eating starfish that consumes vast swaths of the reef. In addition, surges of higher water temperature passing over the coral lead to die-off of the algae that keep coral alive.

Ocean currents have also been affected, and as they shift, fishing suffers—an El Niño year, characterized by warmer temperatures and heavier rains, determines the fortunes of Peruvian anchovy fishermen, whose livelihood is a mainstay of the national economy.

We're all familiar with the continual reports about ice caps melting at both poles, polar bears drowning because they cannot swim the long stretches of open water between the ice floes, and the potential for huge chunks of Antarctic ice cap to break off, melt, and raise the level of the oceans. Low-lying islands like the Maldives in the Indian Ocean are already threatened.

The oceans absorb greenhouse gases as well as heat. Overload the system and the water becomes too acidic (a major factor in dying reefs). Some doomsayers point to the possibility that the Earth's atmosphere might become too poisonous for human life, and this, too, is connected to the oceans.

As fish die, their remains, if not eaten by other fish or the occasional gull, sink to the bottom of the sea, where they rot and give off methane gas. The sea depths are cold enough to trap the methane far below the surface, but with enough warming, the gas will rise and be released into the atmosphere. In sufficient quantities, methane kills living things. The early Earth had large quantities of methane in the atmosphere, which had to come down to acceptable levels before life could emerge. Paleontologists calculate there have been five major extinctions in Earth's history—which, taken together, wiped out not just the dinosaurs, but up to a billion life forms across the five extinctions. The release of methane by the oceans during a warming cycle might be responsible for some of these extinctions.

Whether you are optimistic or pessimistic about humanity's ability to stem climate change, the ocean stands for the totality in one realm of life, and every small effect of climate change stands for the diversity of the human matrix. We can visualize the oceans, map them, observe and measure all kinds of changes in them. But the human matrix reflects the invisible currents of consciousness moving within itself. Unlike the warming seas, which passively react to heat and greenhouse gases, consciousness knows what is happening and invents new responses constantly. This infinite dynamic power is also expressed through you—as with everything pertaining to the totality, this power *is* you.

TOTAL MEDITATION

Lesson 15: Oneness

Once you truly grasp that consciousness is total, you have grasped the secret of infinite power. Oneness sounds abstract. It would be frightening to find yourself floating out at sea with water extending as far as the eye can see in all directions. But the experience of oneness isn't like that. Finding yourself surrounded by consciousness as far as the eye can see is like being at the center of creation. When you are fully awake, your existence will feel exactly that way. (Many religious traditions depict divine beings with eyes all over their body, and there is the all-seeing mystical eye on the one-dollar bill. These images attempt to visualize the state of total awareness.)

There is no pressure to wake up, however. Oneness is already expressing itself through your bodymind. The essential task is to align yourself with totality instead of opposing it. But how do you do so?

You are aligned with Oneness whenever

You enjoy being where you are
You accept yourself without judgment
You feel supported by Nature
Life goes smoothly, without obstacles and
    pushback
Your desires come true with little or no effort
You enjoy being here

You accept yourself without judgment
You feel supported by Nature

The last point might sound confusing, but it is actually the most important. To be supported by Nature is the experience of every living thing. Every creature matches the habitat it lives in. Since this support comes so naturally, a porpoise, an aardvark, an Irish setter, or a rhesus monkey doesn't have to think about Oneness. (It would be nice to know if porpoises do, since they seem to be perpetually smiling.) By the same token, living creatures don't oppose or undermine the support of Nature. However, because humans inhabit a habitat in which choice plays a huge part, we can deviate from the support of Nature.

We do this when

We find ourselves struggling and suffering
We abandon pure food, water, and air
We allow fear and anger to dictate our behavior
We let old habits and conditioning have power
    over us
We forget our role as cocreators of reality

You were born into a world where aligning yourself with Oneness isn't part of a child's training and education. This lack has perpetually left room for much confusion and doubt. If you are not aware that Nature can support you in everything you think, say, and do, it is all too easy to make choices that throw your life off in small and large ways. The solution isn't to put more effort into making better choices, however, because there are always unforeseen consequences. The secret is to align yourself with Oneness—in other words, to practice total meditation.

HIDDEN POWERS

We constantly fail to see how powerful we are. Immersed in the human matrix, our lives proceed within fixed limits. Nothing close to infinite power belongs to us. But the power we could be drawing on is hiding in plain sight. We don't see it because our life is dominated by the voice in our head that is narrating our thoughts. You aren't just casually dropping in on this narration, however. It affects you deeply, and over the years, what you think, you become. That's the problem in a nutshell. Thinking isn't the same as being aware. Quite often thinking—and particularly overthinking—is the enemy of awareness.

Child psychologists inform us that when parents give orders—"Clean up your room," "Turn off the TV," "Go to bed"—their children can easily ignore what's being said. But if a parent says something that describes a child, especially a negative description—"You're not as funny as the other girls," "You're not all that bright," "You're a bad boy"—the words are absorbed and often remembered for life. If these descriptive statements are repeated and backed up with strong emotion, the effect can be devastating. "I am X" becomes embedded in the character of the child, leading to guilt, shame, low self-esteem, and other issues that have no basis except that the words of a parent become the words the child hears in their head.

The voice in your head brings up the past all the time. Even beyond the destructive things the voice might say, being pulled back into the past makes you unconscious of the present. Your mind is elsewhere. Awareness is always present, but if you aren't, then the power of awareness winds up hiding in plain sight, obscured by the screen of thoughts that define "me," the isolated ego personality. Look at the following comparison:

> In awareness *you have unlimited knowledge, infinite possibilities, and an unbreakable connection to pure consciousness.*
>
> In your thoughts *you have limited knowledge, a handful of possibilities, and a faulty connection to pure consciousness.*

Because of this mismatch, it is no wonder that we are forced to rely on the ego—it keeps us anchored to the things we hear in our head, and it keeps our personal story going. "I" feels connected to other people's stories, so we don't feel alone. As long as "I" can hold things together this way, being unaware doesn't seem so bad. You might even overlook it, as most people do.

The voice in your head conspires with the ego to give you a sense of identity. You can see yourself in the mirror as a known quantity, a professional white male in his forties rising up the corporate ladder, for example, or a young woman of color struggling to feed and clothe her children alone. One of those identities is much more desirable in society's eyes, but both feel real and substantial to the person involved.

If you want a better life, your ego sets out to improve the story you are living, and its efforts might succeed. But this kind of success only disguises the fact that the ego was never all that reliable and substantial. It is really just a pack of memories, impressions, likes and dislikes, social conditioning, beliefs, and denial. This pack has been haphazardly assembled with no more structure than newspaper pages drifting down the street in a windstorm, yet it has a way of convincing you that the whole messy assemblage is who you are. Where would you be if you looked at yourself in the mirror and didn't see your ego-based story reflected back at you?

In fact, you'd be much better off.

Nothing that thought produces is a substitute for being aware. The identity you have wrapped around yourself includes much that is false, damaging, and secondhand. As an example, take the sentence "I am not ____ enough." Fill in the blank with a word describing something you think you lack, such as "I am not *intelligent* enough." Other choices might be *confident, thin, attractive, rich,* or *good.* These expressions are not simply self-judgments. They are embedded in your story. The voice in your head is programmed to remember these judgments, which originated in the past when you, or someone in authority like your parents, described you to yourself as not good enough, intelligent enough, attractive enough, and so on.

This discussion makes clear that such embedded self-judgments need to be cleared away. The next part of the book, "Making Your Practice Richer," is devoted to that process. It is just as necessary to replace your story with a conception based on awareness here and now. The self that exists in the present is your true self. It is the self that is connected to total consciousness and always has been. Your true self is the source of all the highest values in human life, and through it you create your rightful place in the human matrix.

There is no need to cling to the false supports provided by ego and the voice in your head. From the moment you begin to wake up, the process of total meditation will reveal your true self. All the doubt, fear, and judgment you have experienced up to now was ego created. It keeps reinforcing your story to serve its own agenda, which is to survive. As you get unstuck from the limitations that seem so real, you will see quite clearly that the ego by its very nature is judgmental, insecure, and afraid.

What makes the whole process of getting unstuck effortless is that you are dismantling a phantom in order to see who you really are. Phantoms can be frightening, but ultimately they have no reality or substance. Everything real and substantial exists in the connection between your true self and the infinite possibilities awaiting in consciousness. It's time to repair that connection so that you can experience reality for yourself.

7

Every Day Awake

It is a radical departure from conventional thought to place everything in consciousness. We all grew up accepting that reality is divided into two separate, very unequal domains. Dominating almost everything was the objective world "out there." This was where the universe began and presumably will end, the same place where billions of people have been born, lived, and died.

By comparison, the subjective world "in here" has created only passing interest. How a person feels is usually considered much less important than what they do to earn a living, raise a family, and try to improve their life. An ill-assorted crew of artists and poets seem to inhabit this inner world instead of just visiting it. Going inward means very little to hard-bitten realists. They approach their inner world to think about practical things and make plans.

If you really look, however, the subjective world also gave rise to saints and sages. Wise beings get their wisdom from the subjective world. Love arises "in here," but so do hate, envy, fear, and anxiety. It is hard to know when your feelings might undermine you, as people well know who have been rejected in love or ended a relationship in bitterness and anger. Of the two domains, the objective one feels solid, predictable, and useful. The subjective world seems fickle, unreliable, and too changeable to really pin down.

Uniting the two domains into a single reality has poor prospects, because the two are so different and even hostile to each other. At work, in battles and emergencies, or just at home trying to get a recalcitrant adolescent to do chores, the watchword is "I don't care how you feel. Get it done." But achieving unity is the key concept behind total meditation. In any given situation you are going to react either consciously or unconsciously. It doesn't matter whether the situation is external (losing an Internet connection, getting a flat tire, catching up on paying your bills) or internal (feeling depressed, worrying about money, missing your child away from home). Any experience you have involves your mind, and your mind expresses your state of awareness.

There is an easy way to label all of this: When you act unconsciously, you are asleep. When you act consciously, you are awake. These labels simplify matters by making it clear you always have a choice between the two. No one is fully asleep or awake, but we can lay out the differences pretty clearly.

ASLEEP
Being Unconscious

You act out of habit.

You obey sudden impulses.

You speak without thinking.

You rely on fixed beliefs and opinions.

You react reflexively.

You have decided in advance what you like and don't like.

You are beset by unforeseen consequences.

You embrace conformity.

You arrive at snap judgments.

You wrestle with anger, fear, and other negative emotions.

You deny things you don't want to face.

Reading this list can be daunting. It can come as a shock to realize that you are probably not as conscious, mature, thoughtful, and rational as you give yourself credit for. Often you are simply asleep. Moreover, if you reflect on any item on the list, you must concede that changing even one of these behaviors is a challenge. But everyone also has experiences that indicate how awake they are, as follows.

AWAKE
Being Conscious

You think before you speak.

You weigh your options before making a decision.

You collect facts.

You anticipate the consequences of your actions.

You listen to what other people have to say.

You feel your emotions but don't always act on them.

You have impulse control.

You plan ahead.

You are open to revising a plan when the situation changes.

You understand human nature and therefore are more tolerant.

You don't jump to conclusions.

You are nonjudgmental.

You balance conformity with the right to be different.

You keep your antennae out for the situation around you and the people in it.

You pay attention.

You can focus steadily on a problem.

A glance at this long list reveals that being awake is much better than being asleep. In fact, many of us spend so much time being conscious, despite lapses into habit and mindlessness, that enlightenment isn't as far away as most people assume—not so far away that they can't imagine that enlightenment is a realistic goal for anyone who wants to live in the world. Quite the opposite is true. Everyone can be shown how to move into a state of greater awareness, and once this process begins, becoming fully awake— the true meaning of enlightenment—is achievable and realistic.

If a human being could be robotized, it would be optimal to write its software program so that every action would come from an aware state. But such a software program can never be written, because a robot makes choices based on predetermined instructions. Being awake is the opposite of being predetermined. When you are awake, you freely choose among infinite possibilities. Ideally, you create your reality on the wings of inspiration and insight the moment these arise. By their very nature, inspiration and insight are unpredictable.

The awakened life makes all kinds of things clear that would be confusing if you are asleep—parenting, for example. As a good parent you are aware that you are an adult, whereas a not-so-good parent sometimes acts like a child or adolescent, unaware this is happening. No one grows up with perfect parenting, but if your parents lacked awareness, they most likely didn't give their children clear directions about certain basic necessities such as the importance of reading and writing, of eating your vegetables instead of snacking on junk food, of getting along with others instead of lashing out emotionally, and everything else that an aware adult has no doubts about.

Childhood development depends upon a stable parent whose actions aren't childish. If a mother threw a tantrum every time her two-year-old threw a tantrum, or if a father shrugged it off when he saw his child stealing cookies from the cookie jar, parenting would collapse into disarray and mixed messages. As it is, psychologists have discovered that "good-enough parenting" is about the best a child can hope to receive. Unfortunately, the world is populated with mothers and fathers who often act from a place of unconscious behavior, with too many holdovers from their own imperfect parents.

Good-enough parents pass along a mixture of good and bad lessons, which is inevitable because they can only act from their own level of awareness. Beyond this they are as asleep and adrift as anyone else, including you and me. We'd all be kinder, and more realistic, toward our parents if we accepted the axiom that you cannot ask of someone what they don't have to give. Fewer axioms are as true or as helpful.

Total meditation will bring you from asleep to awake, but this awakening doesn't happen by addressing every item on the list of unconscious behaviors one by one. Asleep and awake are completely different states, and the challenge is to exchange one for the other. What's needed is transformation. Since even small behavioral changes are difficult, what are the chances that transformation, which involves the entire bodymind, is possible? Transformation is the most important challenge of total meditation.

TOTAL MEDITATION
Lesson 16: Transformation

The awakened life involves no small or incremental change, but rather something more radical and complete: transformation. It takes vision and commitment to believe that such a thing is even possible. Most people have mixed feelings about how their life is going. "Taking the bitter with the sweet," an English saying that dates back to the thirteenth century, expresses a universal experience in every society.

However, in the face of life's mixed blessings there runs a contrary trend, based on a deep yearning for transformation. The yearning is expressed in religion through visions of a Heaven, where eternal bliss is gained; in romantic literature through its vision of perfect love; and in imaginary utopias of every kind, including a lost Eden or a golden age.

Is this yearning for transformation mere wish fulfillment, like dreaming of what you'd do if you won the lottery? If you are totally pragmatic, you abandon such fantasies so that you can productively direct your energies to becoming better off by inches and degrees. (At least one bestseller promises how to get 10 percent happier, which sounds like opening a passbook savings account—better to get a small safe return than shoot for a higher but much riskier reward.) Even then, modest goals aren't always achievable. We settle for half a loaf, or less, because common sense tells us to.

But the real issue runs deeper. Transformation exists throughout Nature. Consider the total change of state that occurs when two invisible combustible gases, oxygen and hydrogen, combine to form a liquid, water, which is so noncombustible that it puts out fires. The essential nature of the two ingredients gives no hint that they could be transformed so completely. But that is what transformation means, as opposed to gradual stepwise change.

What would it mean to achieve personal transformation? Despite the stubborn way that people resist change—clinging to beliefs, fears, biases, and personal habits for no rational reason—we are transformative beings, as can been seen in everyday experience.

- When you have a thought, mental silence is transformed into a voice in your head.
- When you see an object, invisible electrical signals in your brain transform the object into color and shape.
- The sense of sight works by taking minuscule snapshots that individually have no motion, but your mind transforms these into the moving world, the same way a movie is created out of a series of still frames projected in rapid sequence.

- In the presence of a sudden shock, the balanced state of your body at rest is transformed into the aroused state of fight or flight.
- The words "I love you," if spoken by the right person at the right time, create a total psychological transformation known as falling in love.

None of these experiences happens through gradual or stepwise change. Instead, a sudden alteration turns one state into another completely different state. And as with water and salt, the first state gives no clue about what the new state will be like. That's why someone falling in love for the first time often says in amazement, "I never knew such a thing existed."

Why, then, does transformation seem so unlikely and remote? The answer lies in our attitude toward change. Obviously, the setup of society is drastically tilted toward conformity, routine, and conventionality. We feel a pressure not to be different. But none of this alters the fact that we are surrounded by transformation in Nature. Moreover, our brain couldn't change the raw signals received by the five senses into the image of a three-dimensional world without transforming them.

The lesson here is to accept that transformation is always within reach and requires no special effort or struggle to achieve it.

"WHAT SHOULD I DO?"

Human beings aren't fulfilled simply by getting what they want in the external world. Just as important is inner fulfillment. A lifestyle devoted to consciousness attains both. This is an appealing prospect, yet many people, probably most, will wonder, "What should I do?" The answer is this: *Live as if you are already fully awake.* If you were fully awake, the following truths would be completely obvious:

> *Everything in your life is an expression of consciousness.*
>
> *You directly tap into your source, which is pure consciousness.*
>
> *You have attained perfect dynamic balance.*
>
> *You trust that your impulses and desires are good for you.*
>
> *You create your personal reality.*
>
> *Your life springs at every moment from infinite possibilities.*

In a kind of cosmic "fake it until you make it," living according to these truths is much better than waiting for enlightenment to reveal them. They are true beyond anyone's limited perception, just as ultraviolet light is beyond our perception. We wear sunblock anyway. The force of a high-speed impact is beyond our perception, but we wear seat belts anyway. Because everyone's life is mixed, you are already awake some of the time. The trick is to catch yourself when you are asleep—that is, acting unconsciously.

Surprisingly, here is where the divided self turns out to be helpful, because, mentally speaking, we're all used to being in two places at once. We divide our attention all the time, in fact. We pretend to be listening when we're thinking of something else. We hide a sexual impulse at times when we're supposed to be acting like a rational adult. We disguise our aversion to someone by acting polite and friendly. Daydreaming, fantasy, and wishful thinking drift in and out of whatever else we are doing.

This talent for dividing our attention comes in useful when it serves waking up. You favor being aware simply by noticing that you've slipped into two places at once. Once you notice this, it takes no effort to snap into wakefulness. By favoring wakefulness many times a day, you retrain the bodymind gently, but repeatedly, until finally it becomes natural to remain conscious. You'll be surprised at the wide range of small things you can do that are basically effortless, yet immediately effective.

THE EASIEST WAYS TO WAKE UP

When your mind drifts off, bring it back into focus.

When you notice a subtle feeling or sensation in your body, let your attention go there.

When you sense stress in a situation, get away as soon as possible.

When you feel out of balance, center yourself.

When your mind is frazzled, seek a place of quiet and calm.

When you hear yourself opposing and resisting, pause to reconsider the situation.

When you feel dislike or aversion, take responsibility for your feelings.

When you realize you are causing someone else distress, stop doing whatever it is you are doing.

When you feel totally certain, let others speak up and have their say.

When the urge to be in control is strong, consider if you like being controlled.

When tempers run high, make no decisions until they settle down.

When in doubt, postpone making any choice.

When you want to defend yourself, face your own insecurity.

When you feel you must win, stop seeing the situation as competitive—try cooperation instead.

When you are about to show that you are right, consider how you feel when someone points out that you're wrong.

When you bristle at criticism, assume that it is probably justified.

In all of these choices you are starting to act as if you are already fully awake, and for that moment, you are. I don't want the word *easy* to be misleading. If you are in the habit of being in control or always thinking you are right, a fixed behavior won't be amenable to easy change. But you can be aware that you have that behavior and then take a pause instead of going where your habit wants you to go. (Chapter 5, "Getting Unstuck" [pages 129–143], discusses how to change all kinds of stubborn, fixed behavior—we all suffer from them.)

Without training or trying to be perfect every time, anyone can flick the switch from asleep to awake. There is nothing new to learn, even though it takes steady, attentive repetition to get out of the habit of being unconscious. Being awake is our natural state. Your cells already know this, and it helps to be clear about how awake every cell actually is.

Let me offer a detailed example: In the womb, heart cells begin to form eighteen or nineteen days after the ovum is fertilized. Peering at a living embryo in the womb through ultrasound, a trained eye can detect the pulsations of the heart as it begins to acquire its identity. But that's because a cell biologist knows what to look for. If you can imagine yourself as the first heart cell, things would look very different. Two weeks ago you didn't exist. When you came into being, you were part of a cellular blob riddled with electrical and chemical signals flying around in a seeming chaos. Not only did you not know what your eventual role would be, there was no one outside yourself to tell you.

Your identity as a heart cell dawned on its own, and you found yourself transforming inexorably. It didn't occur to you to resist. Some tiny part of you, the DNA in your nucleus, knew more than you did, but it only revealed what you needed to know at this moment. In the larger scheme, the task ahead was tremendous, beyond imagining. To form a baby's two trillion cells, the original fertilized egg needed to divide not millions of times, or thousands or hundreds of times. It needed only around forty cell divisions to go from blob to heart, brain, lungs, liver, and everything else.

As a heart cell, you are fortunate not to look ahead and see that in an average lifetime you would need to beat approximately 80 times a minute and 115,000 times a day, amounting to 3.36 billion beats if you live to be eighty. With advanced engineering, very efficient pumps can be designed out of plastic and metal, but nothing close to the pumping power of a heart, which is why decades of trying to develop an artificial heart have failed to keep a dying patient alive for more than a few hours or days after the device is implanted in the body.

Preparing for its arduous life—a healthy heart pumps more than 2,000 gallons of blood a day—a developing heart cell acquires overlapping functions. Besides its pumping action, the embryonic heart has to build four chambers (two ventricles and two auricles) plus their attendant valves; fashion coronary arteries to bring oxygenated blood to itself; learn to use electrical impulses to coordinate a unified heartbeat; and connect via the central nervous system to receive messaging about everything the brain wants it to do.

Translate this model into your personal life, with its many overlapping processes, and the parallels are strikingly similar. You need to live in the present moment with certainty about your purpose. You need to allow life to unfold without knowing in advance what the future holds. You need to trust that, at some level, consciousness is taking you in the right direction. These are the basics, the foundation, of being awake.

In one important regard, however, your personal life departs from the life of a heart cell. The operations of the heart are complex enough to fill medical textbooks, but heart cells are forbidden to wander away from the biological template that binds them in place. You, on the other hand, do nothing but wander—you invent your own path according to the choices you make. There is no template for being human. That's why in many Eastern spiritual traditions the physical body is called a "vehicle." Like a boat or car, it gets you where you want to go, serving the purposes laid out by desire, aspiration, wishes, fears, anticipation, and expectation—all those jumbled impulses that lie behind all the wandering you do, and will continue to do over a lifetime.

Turning life's bewildering disarray into something organized and meaningful is a challenge, and you confront it at every moment. By the time today is over, you will have decided dozens of times whether to be awake or asleep. Every fiber of your being is set up to respond to your slightest intention. This has been true since the day of conception. Total consciousness has always been there. Development in the womb took place as a whole process, not a piecemeal one. Even as heart cells were differentiating from brain cells and liver cells, they all kept in touch with one another, intimately and intricately.

Nature's ability to protect orderliness and keep chaos at bay is nearly miraculous. The margin of error is microscopic. If heart cells cease being in perfect communication, a unified heartbeat can turn into the writhing chaos pulsation known as fibrillation. It is one of the most frightening things a cardiologist can possibly observe, because within a few minutes the heart literally commits suicide. But the heart has fail-safe mechanisms to prevent such a catastrophe, and leniency is also built into the system, which is why it is generally harmless when your heart skips a beat or you happen to have a benign heart murmur.

Applying the orderliness of the heart to yourself, you can live your life with considerable disorder without immediate repercussions. In fact, the leniency of consciousness is practically unlimited. Chain smokers who keep a constant stream of carcinogens flowing into their lungs are 85 to 90 percent unlikely to develop lung cancer. The oldest person on record, a French woman named Jeanne Calment, was introduced to smoking by her husband. Never a chain smoker, she had a cigarette or cigar after meals until she was 117. And after giving up the habit, she lived another five years. Of course, this is not the norm. The point I'm underscoring is that consciousness is so adaptable that human beings are equipped to survive under the most adverse, sometimes crippling, conditions. Consciousness looks out for us even when we don't look out for ourselves.

TOTAL MEDITATION
Lesson 17: Noticing

"You cannot change what you are not aware of" is an axiom that appears repeatedly in this book. To be aware is also called being mindful. It is very desirable to be mindful. It keeps you in the present moment. It involves being alert and open to new experiences. Mindfulness is also detached: you are open to the present moment but are not attached to any outcome that you desire or fear.

Yet mindfulness has a built-in paradox. How do you remind yourself to be mindful when you have drifted away from the present moment? It takes mindfulness to notice that you have drifted off, yet mindfulness is the very state you are not in. Telling someone to be mindful is like saying "Don't forget to remember."

Fortunately, you can get past this built-in paradox. Your mind is designed to notice things, including unconscious things. Most people are good at waking up at a given time in the morning without an alarm clock. The mind notices what time it is even when you are asleep.

We are so used to inhabiting the thinking mind that we don't see how much consciousness does that isn't thinking. When you notice a friend in the crowd or something appetizing on a restaurant menu or an attractive stranger, what actually happens? You flick a switch and start to pay attention. The thing you notice is selected from lots of other things you are not noticing. When you see a friend in the crowd, you ignore the other people around.

Flicking a switch sounds simple, but noticing can be extremely powerful. Consider the following examples:

- In 1928, the Scottish medical researcher Alexander Fleming returns from vacation and discovers, to his annoyance, that green mold has spoiled some open dishes of cultured bacteria. Instead of throwing the tainted specimens out, he notices that the bacterial cultures have been killed by the mold. Noticing becomes the "Aha!" moment that leads to the discovery of penicillin.

- Because it is impossible to know with any certainty when a piece of stone was quarried, the date when Stonehenge was built is lost in time, nor could anyone figure out why prehistoric people in Britain erected it. Bafflement continued for centuries until the 1960s, when the British-born American astronomer Gerald Hawkins noticed that the lineup of stones could serve to monitor astronomical events like equinoxes, solstices, and eclipses. Although controversial, this burst of inspiration became a viable explanation for Stonehenge's existence.

These two examples show that behind the simple act of noticing, there's an agenda. We do not notice at random. Instead, we notice

Something we're looking for
Something we judge against
Something we fear
Something we might be attracted to
Something that offers an explanation or solution

These are the ingredients in everyone's agenda, even though no two agendas match. Total meditation has its own agenda, which is evolutionary. Its agenda is directed at being aware, which means that you notice opportunities to be more conscious. Catching yourself falling asleep and doing something unconsciously is an important part of this agenda. But there are also other dimensions of the total meditation agenda:

- Notice when someone else needs attention and appreciation.
- Notice an opportunity to give or be of service.
- Notice an opportunity to be kind.
- Notice when help is needed.
- Notice beauty in Nature.

Setting your inner agenda to take advantage of such opportunities helps reset your deeper awareness. Like the internal clock that notices what time it is even when you are asleep, deeper levels of consciousness know much more than your thinking mind does. In particular, your deeper awareness is the source of the most valued things in human existence: love, compassion, creativity, curiosity, discovery, intelligence, and evolution.

Set your agenda to any of these things and it will turn into opportunities that you begin to notice more and more. Alexander Fleming was primed to discover penicillin because he was already a noted researcher with important findings to his credit. A loving mother is already primed to notice if her child feels unwell, something that might escape the attention of a negligent parent.

To notice is to open the door of awareness. What you do after that is up to you. In total meditation you notice much more than you did before, but there is no obligation to act in a certain away. Consciousness can accomplish anything, but consciousness is its own reward.

In the yogic tradition, awareness is used primarily for three ends: devotion, action, and knowledge. Capping these is Raj Yoga, the "king of yoga," which has no specific aim or object. Raj Yoga attains total wakefulness for its own sake, whatever may come. A life in freedom needs no other justification.

In daily life, shifting your inner agenda also involves getting past the kind of noticing that doesn't serve your personal evolution. Noticing other people's faults, being on the lookout to correct someone else, assigning to ourselves the role of rule enforcer, or judging people as winners or losers are wrong uses of noticing. There's no getting around the fact that agendas have a dark side. It is hard to notice something without immediately judging it.

In total meditation, it is important to be aware of your judgments but not to act on them. We are all too practiced in likes and dislikes, acceptance and rejection, attraction and aversion. These opposites dominate our inner agendas. But simply by favoring a new agenda, you can change, and in time what you notice will more and more be self-enhancing. Freedom from judgment begins by not favoring judgments you know are negative. Noticing isn't random. You can begin right now to notice opportunities to wake up. This alone is enough to greatly accelerate your personal evolution.

THERE IS NO PLAN

The future is unknown and unpredictable, whether you look ahead in terms of decades, years, or minutes. Your next thought is as unknown as what the world will be like a century from now. Facing the unknown, we keep making plans, some of which work out, but even this is unpredictable. We can take another perspective, however. Life can be planned by grasping a fundamental truth: There is no plan. At some level, we all realize this instinctively, and our response isn't unqualified joy. "No plan" means that you face the unknown all the time. Is that a creative opportunity or a source of fear?

As with almost everything else in life, opposites coexist uneasily. We are happy and fearful at the same time, never settling permanently on one or the other. We are also free and bounded at the same time, which is why we insist upon being individuals, an expression of freedom, while also conforming in order to fit into society, an expression of being bounded. Not fitting in implies the threat of punishment, as every pained adolescent knows when being bullied on Facebook. No matter how afraid, uncertain, or doubtful we feel, we put on a face that hides those unwelcome feelings. Human beings have a boundless ability to be two things at once. In a totalitarian state, the citizens live in utter fear while marching in praise of a "dear leader."

A classic among self-help books is Susan Jeffers's *Feel the Fear and Do It Anyway*. As a slogan this is good advice, but people quite often feel the fear and run away, don't feel the fear, or refuse to acknowledge that they are ever afraid. In other words, we constantly compensate. We devise workarounds in order to live with, not just fear, but every kind of unwanted experience. Putting on a good face is only the beginning; we can work around a bad situation so convincingly that we fool ourselves into believing we are actually happy. Consider the number of marriages in which one spouse believes everything is going along nicely while the other thinks every day about walking out.

Much of this compromise, conformity, and compensatory behavior would be unnecessary if we accepted, once and for all, that there is no plan. The unknown stares us in the face at every moment. Either you turn this fact into a source of optimism, creativity, and joy, or you face a lifetime of compensating for feelings you can't escape and insecurity that never relents. Your heart cannot predict when it will be racing or slowing down. Your lungs can't predict when they might be gasping for oxygen or gliding along in complete relaxation. Even for them, outfitted with a fixed template of behavior, there is no plan.

Yet on the horizon of the unknown there is a possibility open only to *Homo sapiens*—waking up. When you are fully conscious, you don't fear the unknown because it doesn't exist as either a threat or an opportunity. Those words belong in the field of opposites, an either-or world we inhabit through sheer inertia. The human mind is trained to accept and reject, to feel attraction and repulsion, to judge other people (and oneself) as good or bad. "No plan" means that you are free from such training, which serves only to make life as predictable as possible.

Desire for predictability should be confined where it belongs, to things like the weather, the flow of electricity to our home, the reliability of household appliances. Extending predictability to the human mind falsifies reality. We are designed to freely think, imagine, create, explore, discover, and evolve. Any limitation placed on these freedoms is self-created and self-defeating. The most basic reason for living as if you are fully awake is that you already are—you just don't know it yet. The mind hides from the mind. It creates boundaries and then feels trapped inside them, forgetting that whatever it has created it can uncreate.

That's the paradox that total meditation untangles. Out of the bewildering disarray of life, you can wake up to clarity and certainty, beginning with clarity about who you really are and what you are here to achieve.

TOTAL MEDITATION
Lesson 18: Spontaneity

Total freedom is the goal of total meditation. As we usually understand the word *free*, however, there are severe limits. Some experiences frighten or distress us. We tell ourselves that many things are beyond our reach.

There is a wide gap between limited freedom and total freedom. The first is based on what you can reasonably expect from life. The second begins by looking on life as a field of infinite possibilities. It takes some persuasion to make total freedom seem like more than a pipe dream. Is it even desirable to feel unbounded? The result could be a delusion or lead to anarchy.

Being human, we are divided between what we want to do and what we think we can get away with. No other creature feels this kind of uncertainty. If a tame tiger turns on its trainer and attacks it, inflicting mortal injury, the animal feels no remorse. Only in human eyes did the tiger turn from good to bad. Nothing this threatening is part of daily life for most of us, but we are still constantly negotiating with our desires, following some and suppressing others.

The issue is spontaneity. Society's default position is to distrust spontaneous behavior and pass laws and rules against it. Rule enforcement is the surest way to keep people in line, or so the rule enforcers believe. It is possible to carry this attitude to almost unimaginable extremes. In America, when you go to a bank and apply for a loan, the usual procedure is for the bank to check your credit rating, income, and credit card debt. In China, however, electronic lending agencies check you out electronically, using data stored in the cloud. An applicant using a smartphone gets accepted or rejected for a loan in one-tenth of a second, after the lending agency has checked out 5,000 (!) personal factors, including how firmly your hand moved when you filled out your application and how low you let your phone battery get before recharging it.

Each of us is happy to enforce rules upon ourselves—we don't need an authority figure to do it for us. Self-discipline and impulse control are considered desirable as marks of a mature adult. There's a famous experiment in child psychology in which a youngster is placed in a chair with a marshmallow on a table in front of them. The child is told they can eat the marshmallow right now, but if they wait five minutes, they will be given two marshmallows. The experimenter then leaves the room and watches what unfolds through a two-way mirror. Some children fidget, fighting the impulse for immediate gratification. Others grab the marshmallow instantly or wait patiently until the five minutes is up. (You can view their behavior on an endearing YouTube video, "The Marshmallow Test.")

This experiment implies that we already have a predisposition toward impulse control (or not) from a very early age. The fact that the reward goes to the child with self-control indicates where society wants behavior to go. However, many of life's greatest gifts involve spontaneity, including falling in love, appreciating beauty, composing music, making art, being surprised with "Aha!" moments, and having so-called peak experiences.

How can we make spontaneity be life-enhancing without the need to suppress it? We all police our impulses out of fear, worrying that a spontaneous impulse will lead to embarrassment, rejection, shame, or guilt. These are powerful survival mechanisms in the human psyche. Minor infractions like dropping a piece of chewing gum on the pavement can lead to serious consequences in Singapore (a paradise for obeying rules), while advanced digital technology in China has led to an experiment in which the faces of jaywalkers immediately appear on a public screen, to encourage shaming by others.

Everyone strikes a balance between "everything is permitted" and "everything is forbidden," without really knowing where the boundaries should be drawn. Vacationing at a nude beach is one person's idea of freedom in the sun and another person's idea of public humiliation. Eating five hot dogs at a sitting indicates a serious lapse of impulse control to most people, but in 2018 a man set a new world record by consuming seventy-four hot dogs in ten minutes at a Coney Island contest. ("I was feeling good today," the winner announced happily minutes after downing 21,000 calories of food.)

The solution to our inner conflict is to allow spontaneity to be spontaneous rather than restricted. Such spontaneity is possible only from the level of total consciousness. Otherwise we remain trapped inside self-imposed limitations, obedience to rules, nervousness about being embarrassed or humiliated, and similar worries that are natural when one has spent a lifetime following the ego's agenda. You can't resolve inner conflict at the level of awareness dictated by the divided self.

The war we have with our desires takes place in the divided self. A great deal has to be left behind, because trying to resolve each conflict at a time is pointless and fated to fail. All manner of judgments, beliefs, fear of bad consequences, memories of past embarrassment, and socially trained inhibitions are entangled when we try to decide how spontaneous we want to be. The divided self is wise not to trust itself.

Happily, everyone enjoys enough freedom to enjoy moments of spontaneity, and if we are awake enough, we can experience laughter, joy, and playfulness our entire life (if only this were the norm). The deepest spiritual truth holds that freedom is absolute. When you are settled in yourself and there are no more dark places to fear, nothing hides out of sight. The damaging effect of self-suppression lessens with every step you take to get rid of self-judgment. Bad behavior grows only more enticing when it is forbidden, like leaving the cookie jar out but telling a little child not to grab a cookie. We all know what happens when the mother's back is turned.

Right now you are both your own rule enforcer and a rebel against the rules. It takes a journey into consciousness to become undivided. You are not designed to prosecute and defend yourself at the same time. You are designed so the next thing you want to do is the best thing for you. That's a radical rethinking of what society tells us to believe, but when you adopt a lifestyle based on consciousness, reality will dawn. Spontaneity is the essence of life and the soul of creativity.

MAKING YOUR
PRACTICE RICHER

FEELING THE MIRACLE

10 Simple Exercises

At this moment, if you were fully awake, your life would feel miraculous. Without that feeling, there is no miracle. We should take seriously a famous quote of Einstein's: "There are only two ways to live your life. One is as though nothing is a miracle. The other is as though everything is a miracle." The words are inspiring, but how do you actually live a life with the awareness that everything is a miracle?

Here are ten total meditation exercises to answer that question. In each you are asked to take an everyday experience and see it through new eyes. The aim isn't to connect you to a religious miracle or anything supernatural. The everyday world is miraculous. We are immersed in mysteries at every turn, yet it doesn't matter whether we can explain these miracles. They continue to occur regardless of our viewpoint.

The reason to change your worldview is that you will be drawn closer to your own source in pure consciousness—pure consciousness in its role as the creator of everything that summons the miraculous into our life. Nothing is more basic. If you want to live as if nothing is a miracle, the scientific worldview will back you up. Science is all about taking physical phenomena and giving each the best rational explanation possible. I'm not devaluing the contribution of this approach, because it is obvious that we find ourselves surrounded by advanced technology and all its benefits (as well as its hidden and not-so-hidden dangers).

The problem with the scientific worldview isn't that it strips away the possibility of miracles, although it certainly does that. The problem is that consciousness has had no place in the history of science until very, very recently. Leaving aside the 2010s, in which the "hard problem" of explaining where consciousness comes from began to attract scientific notice, working scientists took two assumptions for granted. The first is that consciousness doesn't need to be explained—it can simply be accepted as a fact of life, like the air we breathe. The second is that if consciousness has to be explained, then doing so within the limits of physical processes will be enough. Basically, the mind will reveal all its secrets once neuroscience maps the brain as completely as possible.

Neither assumption is valid. *You* fall in love, not your brain. *You* have wishes, dreams, beliefs, fears, insights, biases, and curiosity, not your brain. I cannot predict when science will accept that consciousness is the most important aspect of everyone's existence, but without a doubt you and I are totally dependent on consciousness. So that we don't take this fact for granted, it is beneficial to realize, here and now, just how miraculous consciousness is. Only then will you cross the threshold and begin to live as if everything is a miracle.

Try the ten exercises that follow. They are so brief and simple that you can do them all at once or one at a time with a pause to reflect on what you have discovered. Some of the material has been introduced in more detail earlier in this book, but a concentrated dose, combined with your personal experience, makes these meditation exercises really sink in.

MIRACLE #1
LIGHT

Exercise:

Close your eyes and visualize complete blackness. You might use the image of a coal mine or a cave deep in the earth, the night sky without stars, or simply a blackboard. Now open your eyes and look at the room around you.

Where is the miracle?

When your eyes were closed and you imagined nothing but blackness, you were seeing your room as it actually is. No light exists without you to perform the miracle of turning invisible photons into brightness, color, and shape. The night sky actually is black. Stars do not shine. The noonday sky is also black. The sun doesn't shine.

Physics knows that photons are invisible, and photons are the elementary particles that carry light. The fact that we see things happens entirely in consciousness. The brain is as black inside as an underground cave. The visual cortex has no images in it. There is no physical explanation for how the ordinary chemicals that make up the brain—hydrogen, carbon, nitrogen, and oxygen, for the most part—produce the three-dimensional world we see and live in. The whole mystery is the essence of the miraculous nature of the everyday.

MIRACLE #2
TRANSFORMATION

Exercise:

As you sit in your chair, be aware of the air going in and out of your nose. Feel its coolness and the motion of the in and out breaths. Now get a glass of water and take a sip.

Where is the miracle?

The air you breathe is the same as the water you sip. Two gases, oxygen and hydrogen, are present in both (air also contains other gases, principally nitrogen). What makes air different from water is transformation, yet behind this word lies a miracle. There is no rational explanation for why water is wet or why it is the universal solvent. And, as far as we know, there is no explanation for how two invisible gases had the potential to become the one substance without which no life can exist.

Sodium, an unstable metal, and chlorine, a green gas, are separately both deadly poisonous. However, when combined, they form sodium chloride, or table salt, which is not poisonous and which, in fact, is a necessary component of every cell in your body. There is nothing miraculous about sodium atoms bonding with chlorine atoms—the bonding process is elementary chemistry. The miracle is that such simple bonding suddenly transforms two chemicals into something unexpected, inexplicable, and unpredictable. If water didn't exist, it would be impossible to predict that two gases would produce it. If salt didn't exist, there is no predicting that the bonding of two poisons would make one-celled life possible, starting the chain of events that led to *Homo sapiens* and every experience you and I have ever had.

MIRACLE #3
BEAUTY

Exercise:

Look at a photo of someone you find beautiful. It can be a movie star, a baby, or someone you love, but it needs to be a photo and not just an image in your mind's eye. Turn the photo upside down and look at it again.

Where is the miracle?

When you turn the picture of a face upside down, you can no longer recognize who it is. This is a phenomenon related to how the brain recognizes what it sees. The visual cortex is set up so that it recognizes objects in the world right side up. (The fact that we can recognize familiar faces immediately has never been explained, but we will leave this aside as a secondary miracle.)

The miracle is how beauty appears in the face when it is

right side up and disappears when it is upside down. Where did the beauty go? This question cannot be answered without asking where beauty comes from in the first place. It is said that beauty lies in the eye of the beholder, but that is not true—your eyes could not find beauty in the upside-down picture because beauty is a quality of consciousness. We therefore see the abstract quality of beauty differently. The loved one you see as beautiful is likely to be a stranger to me. The special beauty a mother sees in her own baby is more intense than the beauty she sees in her neighbor's baby or in the newborns lined up in a maternity ward.

No one invented beauty. It is something we know without needing to explain where beauty came from. Brain cells process visual images, but only consciousness adds beauty to those images or takes it away. How beauty was born, why it comes and goes, what makes us sensitive to it—all these things are everyday miracles.

MIRACLE #4
LOVE

Exercise:

This exercise requires you to choose something you love, and the choice is up to you. If you really love chocolate, nibble a piece and try to not love it. Make it taste neutral or even distasteful. If there is a movie you really love, imagine it in your mind's eye, recalling a scene or maybe just the movie stars in action.

Now try to hate the movie and think of it as rubbish, a waste of time. You can see how this exercise works. Take anything you love, including the person you love most in the world, and strip away your love so that the thing or person is neutral to you or even an object of distaste.

Where is the miracle?

Once we love something, it is impossible to remove the love. This isn't the same as love turning to hate or a loving relationship that turns sour. We're talking about something you really love right now. The quality of love has merged with the thing you love. It has become like the sweetness of sugar (which is another thing you cannot remove). No one knows how love chooses its object, becomes attached to it, and refuses to let go.

Think of the romances that take a tragic turn. The loved one leaves or dies, and yet for the other person, love never dies. All kinds of complications arise where love is concerned, as we all know. Yet the pure, basic fascination of love has no explanation. You can make a person feel a loving impulse by increasing the amount of certain hormones, but you are only manipulating the sensation of love, which is an isolated aspect. Love in its fullness and completeness reaches infinitely beyond any physical sensation, as evidenced by legends and myths of romance going back thousands of years.

Whether you think of how much you love your pet or how much God might love you, the mystery of love is bound up in consciousness. We are aware of love and always have been, for all of recorded history. Since there is no explanation for why love is universal, it belongs among the miracles of everyday life and is one miracle we can personally feel.

MIRACLE #5
CONNECTION

Exercise:

Think of someone you'd like to connect with. You need to feel that this person is connected to you, so it helps to imagine their face, their voice, or a good memory associated with them. Have the intention of wanting to connect, then wait and see if the person soon gets in touch with you.

Where is the miracle?

This is the only exercise you can't complete immediately. I hit upon it almost by accident. While recording a podcast on Facebook, I asked viewers to imagine someone they'd like to connect with. I posed this exercise as a way of discussing synchronicity, because we've all had the experience of thinking of someone and the next minute having them get in touch out of the blue. It's one of the most familiar ways to recognize the whole phenomenon of synchronicity, which is defined as a meaningful coincidence.

Synchronicity is spontaneous. You don't normally communicate with other people simply by thinking of them. Yet on the morning of this podcast, one viewer after another sent me the same message, "I just thought of a friend I hadn't seen in years, and she just called. Amazing!" I was more than a little surprised. It's risky to ask people to use the power of telepathy, or whatever you want to call it, when telepathy is condemned by skeptics as pure superstition.

In reality, any phenomenon that occurs in consciousness doesn't need our belief or skepticism, approval or disapproval, acceptance or rejection. Consciousness constantly moves within itself. Everything in consciousness is connected, because you cannot subdivide or slice off one aspect of it. Consciousness is whole. In everyday life we act as if we are disconnected, isolated individuals. My mind isn't the same as your mind. But there's a false assumption in that sentence. My thoughts are not your thoughts, but our awareness is the same.

We are connected, first of all, by partaking in human aware-ness. We don't hear what dolphins hear or smell what dogs smell. We don't test the air with our tongues the way snakes do. Within this broad connection there are also specific ties. People share a religion or nationality, for example. Getting more specific, you arrive at family connections. And within family connections, you find identical twins, who are famous for having such inti-mate connections that they can sense what is happening to each other at a distance. There are numerous accounts, for example, of one twin's having sensed the moment the other died.

Connections of this kind go beyond any physical explana-tion. If you are sending out an intention to hear from a friend, and that friend calls you out of the blue, the signal being sent and received isn't a radio signal flying through the air. Connection exists as another miracle of everyday life. To be conscious is to be embedded in total consciousness. There is no separation between you and the whole.

MIRACLE #6
WAKEFULNESS

Exercise:

Sit quietly and be aware of any sensation or thought that comes your way. You can have your eyes open or closed. You can look inward or at your physical surroundings. Now make yourself completely unaware. Blank out everything, right now.

Where is the miracle?

Once you realize that you are aware, you cannot become unaware. In other words, this is an impossible exercise. Once a famous Indian spiritual teacher was asked to prove that there was an afterlife. He gave a surprising reply:

> You are misled in your question. You believe that you were born and will die because your parents told you so when you were a child. In turn they were told the same story by their parents. If you want to know the truth, forget the story and look to your own experience. Can you imagine not existing? Can you feel what it was like before you were born or after you die? No matter how hard

you try, you cannot escape the condition of being
aware. In this lies the secret of eternal life.

In this book and in many spiritual traditions, being awake
and being aware are the same thing. The search for enlightenment is based on being awake and trying to become more
awake. When you stand back, this seems a funny search. Awake
is awake. It exists as a state of consciousness without which you
cannot exist. It is impossible to wipe out awareness no matter
how hard you try. To succeed, you would have to stop existing.

Existing and being awake don't just happen to go together.
They are the same. There are actually two miracles here. The first
is that we are awake at all and not just rocks or zombies. The second is that we know we are awake. The search for enlightenment
isn't about becoming more awake. *It is about acquiring more
knowledge about this miracle of wakefulness.* To know more, you
have to experience more. The experience can involve more love,
more creativity, more compassion, or any other conscious experience. A flash of "Aha!" can bring an overwhelming epiphany.
But nothing of the kind is possible without being awake. Thus
wakefulness is another miracle of everyday life.

MIRACLE #7
REVELATION

Exercise:
This exercise is completely open-ended. Pause for a second
and wait to have your next thought.

Where is the miracle?

Every thought you have ever had, including your next thought, is a revelation. Out of nothing, a light shines. That's a reasonable definition of revelation. There is no need to put a religious spin on the phenomenon. The basic miracle is evident simply by having a thought. Thoughts are unpredictable. No one knows where they come from. Even if you say they come from the brain and point to an MRI of the brain lighting up, that image merely detects gradations of heat and metabolism. Your brain is filled with electrical and chemical activity, none of which is a thought.

If a thought is a revelation, what does it reveal? It reveals itself. Take a simple thought like "The sky is blue." A fact is being stated, but that is only the content of the thought. Before you get the message about the content, the thought announces, "Here I am, your next thought." There is the revelation, that out of nothing, something comes to light. The constant creation of something out of nothing is considered the ultimate mystery about how the universe was created at the Big Bang.

You exist with a thousand small bangs every day, as thoughts, images, sensations, and feelings are revealed to you. You didn't ask for them to exist, and no one knows how "nothing" accomplishes the amazing feat of turning into "something." We stand before it as a total revelation. That's why revelation is another miracle of everyday life.

MIRACLE #8
TRANSCENDENCE

Exercise:

Think of the color pink, and as you do, see the image of pink cotton candy in your mind's eye. Now change the color of the cotton candy to blue, then to green. Finally, see the cotton candy vanish.

Where is the miracle?

You find it quite easy to see an image in your mind's eye and to make it change color or disappear. Instead of taking this ability for granted, reflect a moment. Are you the image of cotton candy that you saw? Obviously not. By manipulating the image in your mind's eye, you have proof that you are not that image. You are beyond it. Likewise, you are beyond any thought you might have. Nothing happening in your mind is you. You pay attention—or not—to what is going on in your mind, but who is paying attention?

The one who is paying attention transcends the mind's constant activity, like a pedestrian waiting on a street corner for the light to change. Traffic and passersby on the sidewalk move constantly, but the pedestrian simply waits and watches. No matter how much they might be attracted by a certain sight, they are beyond the thing they are looking at.

When you saw the cotton candy change color in your mind, something deeper was at work. You created the color you chose. Where did you get the ability to create anything? You didn't go anywhere physically, nor did you open a box of colors in your mind to choose pink. You create mental images simply by being creative; it is an aspect of consciousness that exists nowhere and everywhere. All human beings go there to use their imagination, make a painting, daydream, or recall a memory from the past.

The miracle is that you are here doing a trivial exercise with cotton candy and at the same time you can access pure creativity, which has no location in time and space. In other words, you are timeless anytime you want to be. In fact, you are timeless whether or not you want to be. As a transcendent being, you travel between the finite (time ticking by second by second on the clock) and the infinite (the timeless). Even if you have never seen yourself this way, it qualifies as a miracle of everyday life.

MIRACLE #9
BLISS

Exercise:

In your mind's eye, see a toddler walking unsteadily across the floor. The mother is a few feet away, holding out her arms. The toddler is eager to get to the mother. Their face is wreathed in smiles, their eyes gleam as they rush to embrace her, and at the same time, there is delight in those eyes at being able to walk.

Where is the miracle?

We've all seen a baby's face light up with joy. As you created the image in your mind's eye, the toddler you saw looked blissful. You saw it; you felt it. But whose bliss was it? You assigned it to an imaginary child, and yet you are the one who felt it. In some way the bliss was a projection. It belongs to you, but it also got projected onto the baby.

Any experience of bliss is just like that. The feeling of joy belongs to you, but it is also projected onto something that made you feel joyful. This something can be anything. The English poet William Wordsworth captures the experience of bliss in the following lines from his poem "Surprised by Joy":

> Surprised by joy—impatient as the Wind
> I turned to share the transport—Oh! with whom
> But Thee, long buried in the silent Tomb.

This is actually a specific moment, because Wordsworth has turned to share his joy with his little son, only to remember in the next instant that his son is dead. It is a touching, even a wrenching, moment for him and the reader. Yet what is more uplifting than "unprovoked joy," as psychologists call it? Bliss appears out of nowhere and vanishes of its own accord. It happens to us all the time. We are surprised by a moment of joy, and then it is gone, usually fading away so gently that we don't notice, or perhaps we sigh for a moment when we realize that we are not going to be joyful all the time.

The miracle is that bliss exists in the first place, always ready to surprise us, often when we least expect it. A baby who has no word for bliss, and no thoughts about it coming and going, can tap into bliss anyway. This aspect of consciousness cannot be explained. It just is, a miracle of everyday life.

MIRACLE #10
BEING

Exercise:

See yourself poised to dive off the end of a diving board. You glance down, and below you is not a swimming pool, but rather an ocean of white light. The ocean extends in all directions. The sight pulls at you. You cannot wait to dive into the white light, so you bend your knees, spread your arms out wide, and spring off the board. Now, just at the peak of your dive, freeze the image. See yourself in the pose of a swan dive, frozen in midair above an infinite ocean of white light.

Where is the miracle?

The one thing we are sure of, every single one of us, is that we exist. But this is also the one thing we cannot describe in words. "I am" has no action to it. You can assign all kinds of things to "I am." I am walking, I am hungry, I am a lawyer, I am about to be promoted. But "I am" doesn't need anything added to it. It stands alone.

Yet even those words aren't getting us close to the reality of being. In this exercise you re-created the feeling of a flying dream, which most people would say, if they have ever had flying dreams, feels completely free and ecstatic. Flying dreams liberate us from gravity and fear of falling. But so does being here.

To be is an untouchable condition. In Book II of the Bhagavad Gita, Lord Krishna gives a time-honored description of being: "Weapons cannot cut It, nor can fire burn It; water cannot wet It, nor can wind dry It."

One commentator made the following astute remark about this famous line of verse: "Here the unseen has been explained by means of the seen." If you reflect for a moment, these words describe our entire existence. We act out the unseen, infinite field of pure consciousness by means of the world we see, hear, touch, taste, and smell.

We act out the field of pure consciousness by turning it into thoughts. Poised like a diver in midair over a sea of white light, we are not going anywhere. Being doesn't move, and we are that being. But when consciousness enters the world, we feel ourselves moving, being born, dying, and everything in between. At every moment this is happening, we are poised in midair over the sea of consciousness, which is the sea of Being.

In this last exercise everything is summed up. When you realize that you are an expression of pure consciousness, pure Being, then naturally everything is a miracle. Creation sprang up of its own accord, and you find yourself in its embrace. By any measure, just to be here is miraculous.

7-DAY MEDITATION COURSE:

Insights for Life

INSIGHT AND THE SEVEN GOALS IN LIFE

So far total meditation has made several truths quite clear:

The mind naturally rebalances itself.

When you are balanced, you are in meditation mode.

It takes no effort to achieve inner silence.

Inner silence is meant to be useful.

The last point launches us into this section of the book, which tells you how to make silence personally useful. What drives your life? No matter how different we are from one another, for thousands of years human beings have gotten out of bed in the morning to pursue the same goals and achieve the same dreams. If inner silence is to be useful, it must make these goals attainable and our dreams come true.

WHAT DOES EVERYONE REALLY WANT?

Let me first list the seven basic goals that drive us all:

Safety and security

Success and achievement

Love and belonging

Personal meaning and value

Creativity and discovery

Higher purpose and spirituality

Wholeness and unity

Today, as with every day in the past and every day in the future, you will be pursuing these seven goals. Human nature is complicated, and you are capable of seeking more than one of these goals at the same time. Sometimes they are jumbled together. For example, you can work at a job that makes you feel secure, brings success, and makes you feel worthy. You have found a purpose that includes all three things. If your job is also creative, another dimension is added.

In your marriage or other primary relationship, you naturally want to feel safe and secure. You want the other person to provide love and to make you feel you belong. Is that enough to give your life meaning? For many generations, women were told (by men) that such a life was enough. Now the situation for both men and women is more complicated and confusing than ever.

It helps to clear up some of the confusion by accepting that traditional models no longer define what a relationship should be. Realistically, there is no blueprint for living that fits everyone. The ultimate aim is to fulfill the seven goals in a way that makes them personal. You and your life are one, a unique merger of mind, body, and spirit.

Nothing is achieved in life except through consciousness. You cannot blindly stumble into love, meaning, success, and creativity. Rather, you must evolve into these areas of your consciousness. It would satisfy the logical part of the mind if everything good and useful came in a straight line, but that's not how it works. Children are not seedlings. They don't grow up on schedule to produce apples and roses. Some people sit down and write out "Where I want to be in five years." They may or may not wind up five years later in the place they foresaw. But one thing is certain: The most valuable things in life arrive unpredictably.

INSIGHT MAKES IT HAPPEN

I propose that all seven goals can be achieved. Your true self exists to get you there, following your own unique path. At this moment, your true self is ready to provide anything you need to know in order to reach your goals. This knowledge comes in the form of insight, not just one insight but a whole string of them on a daily basis. Insight can be defined as a moment when you ask for the truth and it is given to you. Consciousness comes alive. Silence becomes useful. The moment can deliver such an important truth that you go "Aha!" You realize your purpose in life or who you want to marry—in other words, the big decisions. But insight doesn't have to be big. Insight is contained in any message from your silent awareness.

If this statement sounds too abstract or idealistic, you need to notice that you have been seeking—and getting—insights from your silent awareness all the time. You dip into silent awareness whenever you do the following:

You ask yourself how you really feel.

You want to know if you should take a relationship to a deeper level of commitment.

You need a bright idea.

You pray for someone or yourself.

You ask an unseen power for higher guidance.

You want to find out how someone else really feels.

You want to figure out how to motivate someone to do what you want.

You are curious about what makes another person tick.

You want clarity about what your life is about and where you are headed.

You want to foresee what lies ahead.

As you can see, everyone engages in the search for insight, and how well your life turns out depends on your skill at seeking your own truth. All the skill you need is already present inside you, because at the level of the true self, you are fully conscious.

A WEEK OF INSIGHTS

Insights come naturally, but not always from the same level. It takes deep insight to fulfill the seven goals of life. Fortunately, deep insight, the kind that allows you to achieve your life goals, is available. Your true self has a clear vision of possibilities that your ego cannot duplicate. Meditation takes you close to your true self. Centered and calm, you make the connection. Now all you have to do is use it.

The insights are there for the asking, but no one taught us how to organize our life by seeking insight. Instead, we make choices based on a jumbled collection of habits, received opinions, social conditioning, and the whole mass of beliefs, experiences, and memories that everyone carries around inside. Insight, however, is almost absurdly easy to learn. You can throw out the confusing jumble of habits, conditioning, and belief right now, simply by going into meditation mode and asking your true self the questions that are actually important for reaching a goal.

THREE QUESTIONS THAT ACTUALLY MATTER

What am I doing right?

What isn't working for me?

What is my next step?

If you had the answers to these three questions whenever you wanted them, your life would thrive. You would grow and evolve. Your cherished goals will be consciously reached. In Sanskrit, you would be in your *dharma*, the path that most naturally and effectively supports your desires.

Since there are seven major goals, it is useful to organize your insight meditations as a seven-day course. In this course your true self is the teacher and you are the student or seeker. There is no set schedule, and in keeping with the main principles of total meditation, you don't need to exert effort. On Day 1, the focus is on safety and security; on Day 2, the focus is on success and achievement; and so on.

The seven-day course is meant to be your constant guide. Ideally it will become a lifestyle. Your true self has a truth to reveal in any situation. Once you learn to seek answers in silent awareness, you will discover that this method is the right way to make choices. The more you organize your week around the seven goals in life, the faster you will achieve them, using the power and knowledge of pure consciousness.

You know yourself better than anyone else does. Through insight meditation you get to know yourself better. As you reflect on the three questions that matter, you are seeking the truth, not simply a casual opinion or a thought you've had many times before. The mind is prone to habit—it gives us mostly the same thoughts over and over. These thoughts are generally good enough to get by with in life, but they don't reveal anything new. Asking for an insight is a conscious process, and once you learn how to do it, the process comes naturally. You'll be astonished by how the world around you reveals itself in new and beautiful ways.

HOW TO ASK FOR INSIGHT

Sit alone in a quiet place and center yourself. Do this by closing your eyes, taking a few deep breaths, and placing your attention in the region of your heart.

You silently pose a question to yourself.

You let go of the question and wait for a response.

You trust that the answer will be given.

At some time, either quickly or later, the response comes spontaneously.

There is nothing arcane about this process. Countless times in our life we stand back and ask, usually in bewilderment, "What am I doing wrong?" or "What should I do next?" Most of the time, however, we don't ask the question in the right frame of mind. We are usually stuck or confused. We've met with resistance and need a way out. The situation is already putting pressure on us, and therefore we are trying to find an answer while feeling stressed. This is what I call being stuck at the level of the problem. Insight meditation is about going to the level of the solution, which is where your true self is located. When you intentionally ask an important question or ask for insight in a relaxed state, you open a doorway to increased consciousness and hence answers are more likely to come to you.

The bodymind is a whole; therefore, insights aren't just mental. You can feel them as sensations. At least one or two of the following will occur.

WHAT AN INSIGHT FEELS LIKE

You are surprised and usually delighted.

There is an "Aha!" moment of making a new discovery.

You feel certainty about your insight.

You feel no need for second guessing or doubts.

The insight has meaning for you.

You feel that you have reached a turning point.

You might feel a physical tingling or lightness.

These indications can help you tell how insights differ from everyday thoughts. The beauty of having your own insight is that it will excite and motivate you. I have said before that the "Aha!" can be so striking that it is life-changing, but a small "aha!" counts, too. Just look for any of these indicators in your meditation, and as time passes, they will become very familiar. You can feel it in your heart and in your bones when you are waking up.

Be alert for changes in perception, too. By this I mean feeling some kind of physical sensation like lightness in your body or pleasant relaxation. Visually, the world around you might look brighter, or familiar sights might suddenly be worth noticing afresh. Keep in mind that such experiences are leading you closer to being awake.

We've covered the basics, so now there's nothing left but to start. You will need patience at first, because looking for insights is something new and for most people very foreign. When you act without insight, you are asleep, and you make many choices unconsciously, which is why your life has fallen into predictable patterns. Thus if you try to ask your true self for an insight out of the blue, the results won't necessarily be forthcoming. There is a gap between "I," the ego personality you have grown accustomed to, and your true self.

To fill in this gap, I've begun each day with a handful of insights to get you started. Some are insights gained from my own journey. Others are the insights of saints, sages, and spiritual guides in the world's wisdom traditions. The words in all these insights come from the true self, which speaks for pure consciousness. Just read them over before you start your meditation, as a way to focus your mind on the goal of the day. I am not asking you to accept them as ready-made insights. Secondhand wisdom is no replacement for firsthand insight.

There is nothing better, however, than aligning yourself with the highest spiritual truths. Generation after generation, they have served to help others to wake up. I always keep in mind a spiritual adage I grew up with in India: "It takes only a spark to burn down the forest." In other words, once you have the first insight about your true self, you will be motivated to wake up completely. Let these meditations be your spark. The flame of enlightenment is waiting to leap up, and you are that flame.

DAY 1: SAFETY AND SECURITY

YOUR GOAL: To feel completely safe and secure

Today's Insights:

> *You are only as safe as you feel.*
>
> *Your true self is never under threat.*
>
> *The world reflects your inner safety or inner insecurity.*
>
> *When you are whole, you are totally safe.*
>
> *To be safe is to be present here and now.*

At the level of the true self you are perfectly safe and secure. There is no threat that can shake your true self from this knowledge, because it is innate, coming directly from pure consciousness. Obviously, everyday life brings situations that feel the exact opposite. The news is filled with stories about disaster and imminent danger. Worst-case scenarios run through our mind when we feel threatened. Stress itself is a threat, even in small doses, because it triggers the stress response, which we inherited as a way to cope with threats by running away (flight) or physically standing up to danger (fight).

A breakthrough occurs in total meditation, because you begin to experience the truth: Being safe is a state of awareness. Today you can get closer to living in a state of awareness that makes you totally safe and secure.

THE THREE QUESTIONS THAT MATTER

Today you can promote your safety and security by reflecting on the three questions that matter. It will probably be most effective simply to choose one question. Let your attention be attracted to the issues that are calling out to you personally.

WHAT AM I DOING RIGHT?

- Any step that gets you feeling safe *in yourself* is right. The basic move is to go into meditation mode whenever you start to feel pressured or insecure. By doing this, you shift your awareness away from stress.

- Get to a quiet place, take a few deep breaths, and pay attention to your body's signals. When you feel tightness, strain, discomfort, or pain, attend to these sensations. Let your attention go to the area of discomfort as you breathe slowly and evenly. Don't force anything. Be patient and let your awareness ease the discomfort naturally.

- Notice the people around you and their state of awareness. Stress goes viral very easily. You want to minimize how much time you spend with people who feel pressured or put pressure on you.

- We are all in the habit of being fascinated by bad news, natural disasters, and all kinds of catastrophes. Get in the habit of paying the least attention you can to such stories. If they make you feel anxious or unsafe, say silently "I am not in danger here" and wait until you feel safe again.

- Be around people who are secure and confident in themselves. Often they are the quietest, most comforting kind of people.

- Create a surrounding that reflects the state of inner security. Focus on peace and quiet, orderliness, visual beauty, and light.

WHAT ISN'T WORKING FOR ME?

- Any step that makes you feel unsafe *in yourself* isn't working for you.

- Being worried or anxious never resolves a situation. At the first sign of worry, center yourself and find your calmness again.

- Being around insecure, anxious, and defensive people may make you feel stronger or give you the sense that you belong. But this is the wrong kind of belonging. It reinforces the belief that the world is unsafe and you are unsafe in it.

- Dwelling on worst-case scenarios doesn't work. You waste time and energy on something that needlessly takes you out of your inner comfort zone.

- Avoid the urge to justify yourself to others. Being defensive is no protection. The more defensive you are, the more insecure is your inner life.

- Giving in to someone else makes you feel you are not strong enough in yourself. Avoid anyone who doesn't treat you as an equal, with respect and consideration.

- Taking outside threats personally doesn't work to keep you safe. If bad news doesn't actually affect you, send hopeful and compassionate thoughts to those who are affected, then turn your attention to something else.

- Latching on to someone else's strength doesn't work to make you safer. You will become dependent, and whenever you have to stand up for yourself, you will feel self-doubt and insecurity.

- Relying on more money, status, power, or possessions to make you safe doesn't work. You are only hiding from your own fear and insecurity. Make inner security your goal, always.

WHAT IS MY NEXT STEP?

- First priority: Do more of whatever you are doing right. Do less of whatever isn't working for you.

- Visualize white light in the area of your heart. Sit quietly and commune with this light.

- Set aside time to go somewhere that feels totally peaceful and safe. Take sanctuary in this place, shutting out any external threat or pressure. Let the feeling of this place merge with you, so that inside and outside both radiate the same peace.

- Take time to support someone you know who needs help. Bring a sense of comforting, reassuring, and being of service to this person. In this way you share your own inner sense of security. Being an anchor for someone else expresses your inner strength and security.

- Look at your area of greatest stress: work, family, or relationships. Find one way today to reduce the stress. Examples: Talk to a person causing you stress

and calmly ask for help. Avoid office politics by
making yourself available to anyone without taking
sides. Reduce the noise and distraction at home.
Honestly share feelings with your partner, avoiding
accusations and blame.

Your insight today:

_____

_____

_____

_____

_____

DAY 2: SUCCESS AND ACHIEVEMENT

YOUR GOAL: To radiate consciousness through the work you do

Today's Insights:

> *Work expresses your level of awareness. (Work
> broadly includes the main activity that occupies
> you during the day.)*
>
> *Work and life expand together or contract together.*
>
> *The more awareness you bring to work, the more
> fulfilled you will be.*

The work you do represents what you think you deserve.

Being awake is the greatest kind of success.

Work and life bring the same joy when you are awake.

If you bring your true self to work with you, any job will be fulfilling. For most people, Day 2 centers on their occupation, but success applies to retired people and stay-at-home parents as well. At any age, we all seek satisfaction and achievement from the main activity that occupies us every day.

You can find a way every day to expand your awareness, thereby giving work, and daily activity in general, deeper meaning. Through expanded awareness, stress and boredom will be a thing of the past. I'm not painting a fairy-tale picture. The reason that millions of people are stressed, bored, and unfulfilled at work is that they are making their expectations come true. This happens unconsciously for the most part, but if you scratch just beneath the surface, you will find the truth: Work is seen as a place where authority rules and insecurity festers. Bored by their job but afraid of losing it, people lower their head, get to work, and look forward to the weekend.

Not every day and not every job are this bad, of course. There's a natural inclination to make the best of things, and, generally speaking, people like the work they do. Yet even here, the self we bring to work is our social self. It's the image we want to project in order to fit in and get along. All images are artificial. They don't express anything close to the true self. The true self exists so that you can expand your awareness, wake up, and find fulfillment no matter what you are doing.

You have the choice to expand or contract your awareness at work. Nothing prevents you from expressing your true self. In fact, it will be welcomed if you display kindness, empathy, acceptance, respect for everyone, and any other sign of wakefulness. No matter what, your work represents your level of consciousness.

A breakthrough occurs in total meditation, because you begin to experience the truth: Work and life expand together or contract together. There's no getting around this fact. Contracted awareness limits your fulfillment, not just at work but in your whole life. Expanded awareness gives you opportunities to evolve through your work, finding success and fulfillment from the inside out.

THE THREE QUESTIONS THAT MATTER

Today you can promote success and achievement by reflecting on the three questions that matter. It will probably be most effective simply to choose one question. Let your attention be attracted to the issues that are calling out to you personally.

WHAT AM I DOING RIGHT?

- Any step that gets you feeling more fulfilled is right. By going into meditation mode, you experience inner calm and silence, which are really just the threshold of fulfillment, because the true self is already fulfilled.

- Fulfillment is expressed as bliss. Any blissful experience is a mark of success. Put a high value on blissful experiences, and realize that how you feel at work is important.

- Take a moment to be proud of the work you do, and praise someone else's work so that they can have their own share of pride.

- If you notice that you are bored, go into meditation mode and restore your sense of well-being.

- Show empathy for how coworkers or members of your family feel. When you have the impulse to be closer to someone on a personal basis (I am not talking about office romance), be open to the impulse.

- Take a few moments at work or during the day for alone time and downtime. If you have a chance, walk outside in Nature to refresh yourself.

- Stand up and walk around regularly during the day to keep your body feeling energized.

- At meetings, be supportive of plans you genuinely value. Be willing to speak your truth when it has positive value.

- Check in often to see what your feeling level is at work or when you are fully occupied at home. Be

aware of your mood—this is an essential part of
waking up.

- Accept new challenges that expand your contribution
to a project.

WHAT ISN'T WORKING FOR ME?

- Any step that makes you feel blocked, frustrated, and
unfulfilled in your work isn't working for you.

- Passively going along when you actually don't like
what is happening isn't working for you.

- Complaining, gossiping, and engaging in office
politics only increases inner discontent.

- Resist the urge to focus on the demands of your job
by working too many hours and bringing work home
with you. Those habits turn work into a source of
pressure and obligation that has nothing to do with
feeling fulfilled.

- It doesn't help to grit your teeth and plow ahead
at a job you hate just to earn your daily bread. The
only thing you will accomplish is to contract your
awareness, and the more contracted you are, the less
you will be able to break out of the grind.

- Being the hardest worker is productive only if it
makes you feel more worthy and fulfilled. It isn't

working if you feel driven and compelled—you are then treating yourself like a machine.

- Resist the urge to label people as winners and losers. Even if you try to be one of the winners, you will be haunted by the fear that you will become one of the losers.

- If you constantly look forward to the weekend, you are either in the wrong job or working compulsively at the right job. Being compulsive at work will over time make you compulsive in the rest of your life.

WHAT IS MY NEXT STEP?

- First priority: Do more of whatever you are doing right. Do less of whatever isn't working for you.

- Ask someone you trust at work to give you an honest opinion about whether you seem to be fulfilling your potential.

- Ask someone close to you personally if you seem happy about your work and speak of it positively.

- Check for unconscious symptoms of being unfulfilled, such as needing a drink after work, griping about coworkers, looking bored or tired, and rarely if ever talking about your dream goals.

- Have a dream goal, and take a step, however small, toward achieving it.

Your insight today:

_____

_____

_____

_____

DAY 3: LOVE AND BONDING

YOUR GOAL: To experience unconditional love

Today's Insights:

Love is an expression of pure consciousness, which is
eternal.

Your true self transmits unconditional love.

In unconditional love, there is no difference between
you and another.

Love wants to share, and so it is eager to bond with
another.

Devotion is the attitude of unconditional love.

The height of devotion is uninterrupted bliss.

Every moment of bliss gives a glimpse of
unconditional love.

When you live from your true self, unconditional love is yours to give and receive. For this to happen, you must be completely awake. In wakefulness you are always connected to your true self, and so the flow of love never lapses. If you are sometimes awake and sometimes not, love comes and goes. This is natural. There will be lapses when you do not experience love, but any moment of love gives you a glimpse of the goal. Love is therefore one of the most positive paths.

Before you are fully awake, the love you give and the love you receive is conditional. It can change or even be lost from sight. For many people, love becomes a transaction—there is a give-and-take with someone else. The beloved has to satisfy the ego personality of the lover. In meditation mode there is a breakthrough: The give-and-take ends. Instead, you experience yourself as the source of unconditional love. As this realization deepens, you can love another person without dependency or demands. Being enough in yourself, your love is a gift with no strings attached.

Since unconditional love is eternal, it never comes and goes but is always the same. Since you do not have to deserve this unchanging love, it is identified with grace. Whether you call it divine grace or the grace of pure consciousness is up to you. Many people find it easier to be devoted to God because they seek a human form, a divine mother or father, to receive their devotion. In the purest wisdom traditions, God is a form that pure consciousness has taken, and you can choose to experience grace and bliss entirely from your true self. Whatever fills you with love is right for you, because everyone's path to unconditional love is unique. The only thing to remember is that love isn't separate from you. Any lapse of love or loss of love indicates a gap between you and your true self, and in total meditation you can heal this gap permanently. Love's eagerness to bond with another is symbolic of its deepest impulse, which is to reside eternally in the true self.

THE THREE QUESTIONS THAT MATTER

Today you can get closer to unconditional love by reflecting on the three questions that matter. It will probably be most effective simply to choose one question. Let your attention be attracted to the issues that are calling out to you personally.

WHAT AM I DOING RIGHT?

- Any step that gives you a loving experience is right. By going into meditation mode, you experience the impulse of bliss that arises easily from inner silence. Bliss, joy, and ecstasy, however fleeting, are glimpses of unconditional love.

- Take the opportunity to be kind and sympathetic. Because kind behavior asks for nothing in return, it expresses selfless love. Unconditional love is always selfless.

- Devotion is an expression of love. Anyone or anything to which you give your devotion is right for you if it is loving devotion.

- The heart is the most sensitive area of the bodymind where love is concerned. Several times today, place your attention on your heart and rest there to feel its warm, loving radiance. If this warm, loving sensation is slight or even absent, give yourself an experience that brings it back. The best choice is to connect in person with someone you love (the ideal is to do this for at least an hour a day). But any joyful experience of Nature, art, music, children at play, or inspirational writing also nourishes the heart.

- Think of six people, including friends and family, that you feel bonded to. Take time to renew this connection at least once a week, preferably face-to-face or with a phone call.

- Any time you make a connection, give of yourself generously, beginning with a smile and a sympathetic word.

- Radiate the love in your heart. Visualize the person you are sending your love to and see a bond of light connecting you. This heart-to-heart connection is silent and only needs a moment. But at the level of the true self, you are enriching yourself and the other person.

- Send loving thoughts and sympathy to people outside your immediate circle. Do this whenever your heart is touched by their situation. Following this up with loving action is even better. You can offer a silent blessing whenever you feel the impulse, even to a stranger.

- When you notice an unloving thought or impulse that has begun to repeat itself, go into meditation mode, become still inside, and tell the thought that it is no longer needed. Repeat until it fades away, not fighting against the unloving thought but informing it that you are no longer receptive.

WHAT ISN'T WORKING FOR ME?

- Any step that makes you want to withhold your love isn't working for you.

- Isolating yourself makes you isolated from the flow of love you could be experiencing.

- Asking someone else to do what you want in order to get your love won't work in the end. The other person can always find a better bargain from somebody else.

- Neediness doesn't work to get others to love you. However obliging and sympathetic they might be, resentment will begin to mount up.

- If you aren't willing to give of yourself, you cannot experience selfless love, which is what your true self is trying to give you.

- Withholding love, including sex, as a form of revenge will disrupt a loving relationship.

- Meaningless sex is never the path to love. Sexuality can be gratifying on its own, but it acquires meaning, value, and fulfillment when combined with love.

- It doesn't work to ask for love from someone who doesn't have it to give, no matter how much you wish they did.

- If you find it much easier to give love than to receive it, your love is likely based on insecurity. You are compensating for the feeling deep down that you are not lovable.

WHAT IS MY NEXT STEP?

- First priority: Do more of whatever you are doing right. Do less of whatever isn't working for you.

- In a way that is easy for you, express more appreciation to others.

- If you sense a bond forming with someone else, encourage it with affection and sympathy. Don't expect or predict anything. Let the bond develop on its own.

- Let others be who they are without judgment. If you judge against someone else, at least be willing to be neutral. You aren't asked to love everyone you know, but you can stop giving signs of disapproval and withholding love.

- Read inspiring scriptures and poetry that exalts unconditional love. Doing so will renew your vision of eternal love as experienced here on earth.

- Find a way to radiate selfless love through service. Alleviating someone else's loneliness, isolation, or poverty is a step toward unconditional love.

- Begin to notice signs of self-judgment. You do not need to try to love yourself—that is usually just the ego personality trying to bolster its image. Instead, go into meditation mode and let the self-judgment fade away. You don't have to fight it—just stop listening.

Your insight today:

_____

_____

_____

_____

_____

DAY 4: PERSONAL MEANING AND VALUE

YOUR GOAL: To live with certainty about your self-worth

Today's Insights:

Self-worth is achieved by living your truth.

When you look to your true self, your life has meaning.

Every value in your true self adds another layer to your life's meaning.

The ultimate purpose of anyone's life is to be fully conscious.

When you are fully awake, you express every truth.

The meaning of life is found in the present moment and how you respond to it.

Pure consciousness is the reservoir of infinite possibilities, the source of purpose and meaning.

As long as you exist, your life has meaning. Total consciousness is flowing through every cell. The entire universe is conspiring to make the present moment possible. At the level of your true self, the truth of these concepts is very clear. There is no mistaking how worthy you are. Life finds a purpose in every individual simply by your being aware. But when your awareness is limited, self-worth comes into doubt. The ego personality is in a state of disconnect from the true self. Therefore, it always doubts whether it is worthy. To live from the ego is to wonder if you really matter.

In total meditation, the state of inner calm and silence justifies itself. You don't have to work for it or deserve it. The same principle holds true outside meditation mode. If you only realized it, your existence has been meaningful every moment since you were born. Realization is the key. You must see and feel how worthy you are. Most people look in the wrong place for validation. They seek approval outside before they feel self-worth, and if the approval turns to criticism, they are devastated. Being tied to the approval and criticism of others can never achieve lasting, unshakable self-worth.

The ability of the ego personality to feel worthy is shaky and temporary. Typically, "I" looks to externals like money, possessions, and status to prove that it is worthy, but they are a facade. The only times the ego feels genuinely worthy are when it has connected with the values of the true self. Everyone experiences this connection off and on, which demonstrates that the true self is always trying to communicate with us.

That's why we feel impulses of loving kindness, the absence of self-doubt, a desire to show gratitude, and a sense of complete well-being. "I am enough" becomes the underlying attitude no matter what you are doing. By making the connection permanent, which happens once you are completely awake, you find yourself in a unique position. Your life expresses everything that the ego tries to achieve through self-importance. Yet in reality you feel humble and selfless. You have become the instrument of higher consciousness as it radiates its truth in the world.

THE THREE QUESTIONS THAT MATTER

Today you can get closer to unshakable self-worth and meaning by reflecting on the three questions that matter. It will probably be most effective simply to choose one question. Let your attention be attracted to the issues that are calling out to you personally.

WHAT AM I DOING RIGHT?

- Any step that gives you a sense of purpose is right. By going into meditation mode, you experience something very simple and yet all important: a sense of self. No matter what you think, say, feel, or do, your sense of self silently watches and never changes.

- Enjoy being who you are. Take a moment to feel how good it is simply to be here. "I am" is the foundation of the true self.

- Aim for self-reliance in everything: how you feel, the beliefs you express, your work, your role in the family. These things belong to you alone. Appreciate them and give them value.

- Let others praise you and show their appreciation. It may be hard to receive love and praise, but they reflect your inner worth.

- Undertake a project that really means something to you. Self-worth needs to express itself by going out into the world. Silently thinking about how great you could be, or how little you matter, is a sham constructed by the ego. When you immerse yourself in a meaningful project, you allow your inner worth to expand and evolve.

- To be modest and humble about yourself is a sign of great self-esteem when those feelings come from the true self.

- The guiding principle is to respect others as you would respect yourself. This is the true self's natural attitude, because in everyone the true self is equal.

WHAT ISN'T WORKING FOR ME?

- Any step that makes you feel small and insignificant isn't working for you.

- Attaching yourself to someone who is strong and accomplished can be a great experience, but it doesn't add to your self-worth. Most of the time you will only be trying to fill a hole in yourself. Take away that strong person, and the hole will be just as empty as before.

- Making yourself seem big by making others look smaller doesn't work. You won't convince anyone, and your behavior will create resentment. Making someone else your inferior reflects your own insecurity.

- Self-image isn't the same as the true self. Polishing your self-image will satisfy the ego personality while keeping you disconnected from your true self. By its very nature a person's self-image is deceptive, because it masks what lies beneath. The ego thinks it is doing itself some good by hiding what it is ashamed of and doesn't want the public to see. But the greater loss is that self-image hides the true self, which can heal any weakness or wound.

- Trying to make yourself important in other people's eyes doesn't work. They will always have their private opinions of you, fair or unfair. Let others make you great in their eyes, or not. It isn't your job.

WHAT IS MY NEXT STEP?

- First priority: Do more of whatever you are doing right. Do less of whatever isn't working for you.

- In a way that is easy for you, be modest and unassuming. At the level of the true self, pure consciousness has made you what you are, not your ego.

- Being the best you can be is more important than doing the best you can do. It is desirable to do your best, of course, but your being, meaning your state of consciousness, determines your self-worth beyond anything you will ever do.

- Be grateful to your source for every gift it has given you. No one's ego ever created the things we cherish in life.

- If you find yourself repeating the word "I" very often, go into meditation mode and reconnect with who you really are. Your true nature is selfless.

Your insight today:

_____

_____

_____

_____

DAY 5: CREATIVITY AND DISCOVERY

YOUR GOAL: To make your life a journey of discovery

Today's Insights:

As long as you follow your curiosity, you will never grow old.

Renewal is the eternal secret of life.

Anything you pay attention to can reveal a mystery.

When you explore the world, you are really exploring yourself.

Every new discovery is also a self-discovery.

Consciousness by its very nature is creative and curious.

To lead a creative life, be fascinated by change.

Every moment brings you to the threshold of a new discovery.

You were assigned a creative life the moment you were born. The assignment came from consciousness, which by its very nature craves to know and understand. This is why children are so fascinated by the world. They are immersed in the wonder of knowing new things. Life never runs out of new things to show us. Anything you turn your attention to can reveal something you never knew before. But if you stop paying attention, wonder vanishes and life becomes predictable and routine.

Are you afraid of change or fascinated by it? People who resist change are secretly afraid of it (or not so secretly). They are forced to pretend that safety lies in making their life as routine and predictable as possible. This strategy flies in the face of reality, because life is nothing but change. Every day is a new world. Either you wake up to this fact and embrace it or you sentence yourself to constricted awareness, increasing boredom, and becoming tired of your own life.

Your true self sees life as a journey of discovery. It wants to explore all the possibilities that make each day new. There is no secret behind this—your true self is simply expressing the curiosity and wonder you were born with. To be awake is an unpredictable state. It has to be, since consciousness seeks a creative outlet at every moment.

We crave watching the news so eagerly that it is fed to us 24/7 on television and in social media. We can't wait to hear what is happening to other people, yet somehow we don't tune in to the news about ourselves. The ego personality is afraid to look inside too deeply, anxious about what it might discover. To avoid true self-discovery, the ego is telling you a story based on the past. "I" is constructed from old memories. When you get out of bed to repeat the same story you lived yesterday, you are just putting old wine in new bottles, as the saying goes.

To truly renew yourself, the place to start is in meditation mode. When you connect with your true self, every perception feels fresh and new. The true self lives in the present moment, which is the only place where discoveries can be made. The eternal now is the eternal you. That's the most important discovery anyone can make.

THE THREE QUESTIONS THAT MATTER

Today you can renew yourself by reflecting on the three questions that matter. It will probably be most effective simply to choose one question. Let your attention be attracted to the issues that are calling out to you personally.

WHAT AM I DOING RIGHT?

- Any step that follows your sense of curiosity is right. By going into meditation mode, you refresh your mind in silence. Only a fresh mind can have fresh perceptions—this is how all discoveries begin.

- Be open to everyone you meet, without preconceptions or judgments. They are as fascinating as you are to yourself once you open your awareness.

- Get in the habit of paying attention. Life is only boring if you stop paying attention to the newness in every moment.

- At every moment you can be centered in yourself, awaiting the next surprising discovery. Because inner silence is awake, it is constantly aware that something new lies just around the corner.

- When you discover something really meaningful, it feels totally personal. You are seeing yourself reflected in the world "out there." In the end, what delights everyone the most is to find something new in themselves. When something you see makes you suddenly surprised, joyful, or fascinated, you are bringing those qualities of the true self to light.

- It is more important to explore yourself than to explore the world. Every real value in life—truth, beauty, meaning, purpose, love, compassion, or any other spiritual value—awaits in your true self.

Getting more and more in touch with these values in your true self is your goal when you embark on the journey of self-discovery.

WHAT ISN'T WORKING FOR ME?

- Any step that makes you feel that life is boring, routine, and predictable isn't working for you.

- Taking other people for granted doesn't work. You are denying them the capacity to be new, which is the very thing you want for yourself.

- If nothing really interests or excites you anymore, you are living from the level of the ego personality. You have lapsed into routine, because keeping things the same is the ego's primary defense mechanism. A predictable life gives "I" the false sense of being in control. In reality, the ego has settled for a very limited existence.

- Resisting change won't work in the end. You are only bolstering the ego's insecurity and fear. Reality is in the process of eternal change. Once you accept this fact, you can begin to embrace change without anxiety. Resist this fact, and change won't stop producing anxiety.

- Giving in to the people who don't want you to change isn't working. Someone else might want you to be in a box, but the only person who can box you in is yourself. You know you are in a box when you have grown tired of yourself. Your become bored with yourself when you are motivated to go along, fit in, earn the approval of others, and submit to social conventions.

WHAT IS MY NEXT STEP?

- First priority: Do more of whatever you are doing right. Do less of whatever isn't working for you.

- In a way that is easy for you, be more open to new people and experiences.

- Find something new in every relationship. Renewed interest doesn't happen because the other person changes. It happens because you start noticing and paying attention.

- Shrug off the tendency to repeat yourself. The same old thoughts, same old attitudes, and same old choices are symptoms of the same thing: being asleep.

- Take time to relish the light of life. It appears in children, art, music, the wonders of Nature, the light of pure consciousness, and the lightness of being.

Your insight today:

_____

_____

_____

_____

_____

DAY 6: HIGHER PURPOSE AND SPIRITUALITY

YOUR GOAL: To radiate your cherished spiritual values

Today's Insights:

Everyone's higher purpose is to wake up completely.

Higher consciousness and spirituality are the same.

Living in separation is an illusion you can wake up from.

Your connection to pure consciousness is always present.

Your true self radiates divine presence.

Your highest purpose depends on who you are, not what you do.

In your very being you are infinitely valuable.

Every spiritual attainment is found in your true self,
waiting to be awakened.

Your true self radiates every spiritual value you yearn to experience. When you are awakened, you radiate the same values of love, compassion, mercy, empathy, and forgiveness without effort. Already you have had glimpses of these values in yourself. By practicing total meditation you expand these glimpses, making them deeper and more frequent.

In modern life, many people are facing a frustrating dilemma: they yearn for spirituality but feel blocked from leading a spiritual life. As organized religion has become less satisfying in many ways, spirituality has become a lonely venture, filling people with high hopes, but also a kind of shaky uncertainty about the inner journey. In addition, the demands and complexity of everyone's busy life makes it difficult to find time to "be spiritual."

The answer to this dilemma is to remain in your spiritual core all the time, a state of awareness that unfolds through total meditation. There is no real separation between the worldly and the spiritual, even though centuries of organized religion have gotten us into the habit of respecting such a division, even going so far as condemning worldly existence as being contrary to God and devotion. However, everything happens in consciousness. You don't have one consciousness for raising a family, going to work, and buying groceries and another consciousness for praying and carrying out your devotions. The true self expresses the most cherished human values. As viewed from the true self, love is love, devotion is devotion.

Seen this way, the spiritual values people crave to experience are seamlessly woven into everyday life and are accessed simply by being awake. *The more awake you are, the more you will radiate spirit. The true self will shine through everything you do, because doing isn't the important part. The important part is being.* Who you are has more spiritual value than even the most reverent thoughts and deeds. What the true self gives you is presence. We can call it divine presence, but I consider it the presence of pure Being. God and pure Being are both absolute, infinite, all-knowing, and all-powerful—they are simply different names for the source of creation.

The nearer you are to your source, the nearer you are to the source of creation. The two are the same. This fact gives your existence infinite value. You share the true self with anointed saints and sages. Once you accept this as true, the spiritual journey is no longer frustrating and distant. Every glimpse of the true self tells you who you really are, and you don't have to follow an arduous journey to discover it.

THE THREE QUESTIONS THAT MATTER

Today you can live from your spiritual core by reflecting on the three questions that matter. It will probably be most effective simply to choose one question. Let your attention be attracted to the issues that are calling out to you personally.

WHAT AM I DOING RIGHT?

- Any step that makes you feel a spiritual presence in yourself is right. By going into meditation mode, you open a channel for any and all spiritual values to radiate.

- It is right to accept that every person shares a true self, which means that no one is without the potential to express the higher values of love, compassion, and forgiveness. Glimpses of awakening are sent to everyone even if these are not valued as much as they should be.

- Get in the habit of noticing and appreciating any glimpse of your true self. You might even pause to tell yourself, "This is who I really am."

- It is right not to define other people by their behavior, moods, habits, and weaknesses. Everyone suffers from a disconnect with the true self. Be grateful that you are healing your disconnect without judging someone else for theirs.

- Act from your heart as much as you can. This is the surest way to reconnect with your true self. The heart heals wounds and encourages acceptance, which all of us need.

WHAT ISN'T WORKING FOR ME?

- Any step that makes you feel isolated, alone, and insignificant isn't working for you.

- Trying to be spiritual doesn't work. It is no substitute for the true self, which is effortlessly spiritual by its very nature.

- Making someone else feel unworthy doesn't work. You are denying that they have a true self. Be patient and forgiving whenever you can. This is made easier by never forgetting that you are not in perfect connection with your true self either. Everyone is ready for healing.

- It doesn't work to worship a God that is merciless, vengeful, and unforgiving. God is meant to be a model for humanity, and this world would be hellish without grace and mercy.

- If you lose faith that you really matter, you are feeling a disconnect with your true self. You are of infinite worth, needing only to connect with this truth in order to feel it. Keeping faith in your spiritual value is one of the best uses of faith.

WHAT IS MY NEXT STEP?

- First priority: Do more of whatever you are doing right. Do less of whatever isn't working for you.

- Define yourself by the best that is in you. Reject demeaning thoughts. It works to address such thoughts by saying, "I do not need you. This isn't who I really am."

- Humility is a spiritual quality, but self-deprecation isn't. It is a sign that you are judging against yourself. Be sure never to join in any comment or joke that makes you small or less than worthy. Know that you are above both the criticism and the approval of others.

- In a way that is easy for you, make other people feel as valued as you value yourself.

Your insight today:

_____

_____

_____

_____

_____

DAY 7: WHOLENESS AND UNITY

YOUR GOAL: To exist in total freedom and bliss

Today's Insights:

Your true self was never born and never dies.

Being eternal, you are whole. Being unbounded, you are whole.

Being here now is enough. There is nothing more to seek once you realize this.

Pure consciousness is complete, and you are pure consciousness.

Beyond light and dark, good and evil, all opposites melt away. Then your existence is pure bliss.

In wholeness you are free, because there is nothing to oppose you and nothing for you to oppose.

There are many things you can strive for, and life is filled with all kinds of achievements. The one thing you can't strive for is wholeness. Either you are whole or you aren't. Wholeness isn't measured by anything you have ever done or will ever do. Wholeness is something you realize. It is like looking into a spiritual mirror and seeing the truth reflected back at you.

Until you are fully awakened, wholeness is difficult to conceive. We were all trained to live in separation. We split our experiences into pairs of opposites like good and evil, "you" and "me," and all manner of things we like and dislike. The constant activity of accepting X and rejecting Y occupies the ego personality incessantly. There seems to be no choice except to define "I" as a jumble of all the things we accept and reject. As long as you identify with the ego personality, there is no doubt that you will anchor your identity this way.

There is an alternative, however, which can be described simply as "It's all okay." In those three words, freedom is hidden. If everything is okay, there can be an end to struggle, resistance, fear, and limitation. Those things exist only because the ego personality views some things as *not* okay. It is impossible for everything to be okay as long as you identify with "I," and since all of us do identify with "I," reaching a different viewpoint is almost impossible or, at the very least, confusing.

"It's all okay" is the natural state of a healthy body. Every cell is coordinated with every other. All internal processes mesh into one whole. Why is it so hard to translate this wholeness into the rest of life? The answer isn't in blaming human nature or the lamentable condition of the world. Both reflect a state of consciousness that is attuned only to separation. The world proceeds by the clash of opposites because we approach our own life this way.

I realize that the reader might react instinctively against "It's all okay," because we are all conditioned to navigate through the state of separation. We see bad things and want to correct them. We see good things and want to encourage them. It seems only right to live that way, but the whole point of waking up is different and requires a shift internally.

Wholeness is as natural to the mind as it is to the body, because the bodymind is one thing. When either aspect of the bodymind goes into imbalance, it returns to balance of its own accord. The return to wholeness takes time because some imbalances are stuck in place, but the process of returning to wholeness is always with us. Nothing can make imbalances worse, or permanent, except the ego personality.

The hallmarks of wholeness are present in you now. You glimpse wholeness in moments of freedom, calm, settled quiet, and bliss. Bliss stands out in particular, because the other signs are passive. Quiet and calm are the absence of disturbance. Bliss is a vibrant experience. Its joy and ecstasy are unmistakable. As grateful as we are when we receive an experience of bliss, the real goal is permanent, unchanging bliss. Your true self feels it already, and as you wake up, you will merge with your true self and feel that bliss is constant, never to be taken away.

THE THREE QUESTIONS THAT MATTER

Today you can live from your bliss by reflecting on the three questions that matter. It will probably be most effective simply to choose one question. Let your attention be attracted to the issues that are calling out to you personally.

WHAT AM I DOING RIGHT?

- Any step that makes you feel blissful is right. Going into meditation mode makes that possible at will. You can trigger the experience of bliss by sitting quietly and recalling past moments of delight and joy. You are inducing what psychologists call "unprovoked happiness," meaning that you, and not the outside world, are making the bliss happen. Without your realizing it, this has always been true. Bliss occurs in consciousness and nowhere else.

- To be blissful you must have no inner conflict. Inner conflict takes the form of self-doubt, mixed feelings, putting up resistance or feeling resistance from others, and harboring old grievances. Be aware when any of these signs appear, and have the intention that they go away. Don't dwell on them. Stop nursing any grudges you might feel.

- Get in the habit of being inclusive. Wholeness puts up no barriers of rejection, and your true self doesn't either.

- Invent your own form of "follow your bliss." The path to wholeness lies in that direction. Take time every day, and preferably many times a day, to refresh your sense of bliss.

WHAT ISN'T WORKING FOR ME?

- Any step that makes you feel conflicted inside isn't working for you.

- You are inciting conflict by us-versus-them thinking.

- You will be surrounded by conflict if you believe that it is you against the world.

- Believing that happiness is for other people won't work. Happiness is the natural result of feeling "I'm okay." The root cause of your own unhappiness lies in self-judgment.

- Taking the bitter with the sweet is usually a sign that you expect life to be bitter just as often as it is sweet. In your true self there is no bitterness, because bitterness is born of regret and resentment from the past. That the true nature of consciousness is blissful must be kept in mind even when life presents difficulties. One sour apple isn't reason for throwing out the whole harvest.

WHAT IS MY NEXT STEP?

- First priority: Do more of whatever you are doing right. Do less of whatever isn't working for you.

- Define your goal as the highest thing possible, which is freedom and bliss. Celebrate every time you escape a self-imposed limitation.

- Do your best to think about any situation without turning it into winners and losers, us versus them, and other forms of divisiveness. All divisions arise inside you and are abolished inside you.

- Immerse yourself in the world's inspirational literature that expresses ecstasy and freedom. Nothing is quite so powerful as a means to increase your own bliss whenever you wish.

Your insight today:

_____

_____

_____

_____

_____

VIBRATING THE SILENCE

52 Mantras

This section of the book contains fifty-two mantras that can be used as a year's course in mantra meditation or chosen one at a time to spontaneously enrich your inner life. To begin, let us look into the value of a mantra in the first place.

What is the best way to use silence? This question arose thousands of years ago when it was first discovered that silent mind existed. As I've mentioned before, silence is either useful or useless. By itself, it has no special value. The mind has simply stopped its ceaseless activity. But once silence was noticed somewhere in ancient history, a second discovery was made: Silence is more than stasis. It is a state of heightened awareness, and in this state we have special creative opportunities.

In effect, you can create anything from the invisible "stuff" of silence. You have already been using this ability in creating a lifetime of thoughts and feelings. Every idea, whether trivial or earth shattering, emerges from silence. Naturally, one wants the best to emerge. The more creative and life-supporting your thoughts, the better off you will be.

An entire science of vibrations (known in Sanskrit as *shabda*) arose in India specifically to enrich inner silence. The central feature of this science is the mantra, a word used in meditation for its vibrational value. Here the word *vibration* is not quite what we think of when sound vibrations reach the ear. The term is much closer to quantum physics, which reduces all matter and energy to vibrations or waves in the quantum field. Before a cat is a cat, it is made of atoms. The atoms are made up of subatomic particles, and those particles vanish into the quantum field as invisible waves or vibrations.

From this we can see that vibrations are creative, and that is the purpose of a mantra, to create a quality in silence that brings the values of consciousness—love, serenity, compassion, empathy, creativity, and much else—into a person's awareness. By vibrating the silence, mantras enrich a person's inner life, with many consequences in outer life.

HOW TO USE THE MANTRAS

Each mantra is given in two forms: as a mental sound in Sanskrit to repeat silently, and as an affirmation of what the mantra's effect is meant to be. Some of the mantras are as simple as one syllable, like *Om*, which is easy to repeat silently, while others can be five or more syllables long. If you find the longer ones too difficult to remember, feel free to use the affirmation side of the mantra instead.

Since there are fifty-two mantras total, you can go through them systematically, using one for a week at a time for a year. But some people will prefer to open the mantras at random and use whatever mantra comes to light.

Using a mantra is quite simple.

1. Pick the mantra you want to use.

2. Close your eyes and meditate on the mantra for 5 to 10 minutes. The correct pronunciation is given in brackets.

3. Look at the affirmation that goes with the mantra and reflect upon it to align yourself with the mantra's beneficial effect.

You don't need to chant the mantra internally to make a rhythm. Just say the mantra whenever you notice it has gone away. Don't try to squeeze in as many repetitions as you can—it's not effective.

The whole procedure is meant to be relaxed and easy. Just let the mantra be like any other word you bring to mind, letting it go in and out of your awareness on its own. Whatever you are comfortable with will work. There is no wrong way to do mantra meditation.

MORE ABOUT THESE MANTRAS

Mantras are basic sounds in Sanskrit that contain energy and intention to promote spiritual growth. They are a tool for waking up that supports the natural process of spiritual transformation. The inherent intelligence of pure consciousness is at work. As you've learned in this book, your mind naturally wants to go to its source in silent, unbounded awareness. Mantra meditation is a helpful way to add to your time spent in meditation mode.

You've probably heard of people being given one mantra to use as their own. There are actually thousands of different mantras, but these so-called seed, or *bija*, mantras that get assigned personally are a convenient place to begin. *Bija* is the Sanskrit word for seed, and these mantras are the most basic vibrations, or primordial sounds, of pure awareness. They exist and work at a level of the mind much more fundamental than thinking or even feeling.

Because primordial sounds are considered the basic vibrations in Nature, existing before language developed, seed mantras don't represent anything we can think about: they have no distinct meaning. Rather, they are fundamental frequencies of consciousness associated with sound that we can meditate on in a very pure way. For that reason I am beginning with seed mantras. They align one's life to the impulses of creativity and intelligence in Nature.

The later mantras have more specific applications that will be explained for each one. Mantra meditation has amassed the widest and most far-reaching research of any meditation practice. Reductions in anxiety, lowered blood pressure, effective stress management, and other mind-body benefits are now well established. I therefore encourage you to experiment with these mantras—they hold much promise within the larger world of total meditation.

1. OM
[Ohm]

Pure consciousness is the source of creation.

This seed mantra has no specific meaning. It is associated with all-inclusive existence, expressed as the primal vibration *Om*. This is the sound or vibration of consciousness through which all processes in creation are generated.

2. HRIM
[Hreem]

I am truth and joy.

This seed mantra's sound is the energy of consciousness associated with a person's spiritual heart. It radiates a light of truth, strength, love, expansiveness, and happiness.

3. KLIM
[Kleem]

I am the power of love and fulfillment.

This seed mantra's sound is the stream of awareness that is forever creating, nourishing, refreshing, revitalizing, attracting, and delighting. We can call it the energy that fulfills the deepest desires of the heart, not only for love but also for the ultimate fulfillment of waking up.

4. SHRIM

[Shreem]

I am beauty, abundance, and joy.

This seed mantra's sound is the energy of pure consciousness expressing the quality of abundance, nurturing generosity, devotion, enjoyment, beauty, and pleasure. It is a gentle energy that supports the nurturing and caring value in human awareness.

5. HUM

[Hoom]

I am the power of transformation.

This seed mantra's sound expresses the transformative power of awareness. It is visualized as a spiritual fire that illuminates and affirms what is true and enduring while purifying and removing what is false, negative, and transitory.

6. KRIM

[Kreem]

I am the force of evolution.

This seed mantra's sound expresses the organizing power of consciousness. It is the energy that keeps every cell operating and makes thinking orderly. The same energy unites mind and body into one wholeness that grows and evolves.

7. GAM

[Gum]

I am wholeness and harmony.

This seed mantra mantra's sound expands awareness as a way of resolving obstacles and attaining success. Where there is stuckness, this mantra opens awareness to the level of the solution, the level of the true self.

8. AIM

[I'm]

I am creativity and inspiration.

This seed mantra's sound awakens the awareness within that brings success in spiritual understanding, insight, and creative inspiration. It especially helps those involved in learning, teaching, research, art, and music.

9. DUM

[Doom]

I am fearless and strong.

This seed mantra's sound supports the energy of maternal protection, encouragement, strength, and empowerment. It represents the true self that resolves difficulties and overcomes resistance.

10. HAUM

[How'm]

I am open, unlimited awareness.

This seed mantra's sound affirms that your essential nature is not conditioned, limited, or defined by any experience, positive or negative. Your true self remains an unbounded field of possibilities at all times and under all circumstances.

11. AIM KLIM SAUH]

[I'm Kleem Sow (as in a female pig)]

My heart is whole and fulfilled.

This mantra is a combination of sounds for realizing one's heartfelt desires. By renewing the heart, it also resolves long-standing issues of stress, anxiety, pain, and grief.

12. HRIM SHRIM KLEEM

[Hreem Shreem Kleem]

I am wisdom, love, and generosity.

This mantra's sound activates the energy of the spiritual heart in fulfilling your innermost desires. It draws on the quality of pure consciousness that is all-knowing.

13. OM HAUM JUM SAH

[Om How'm Joom Sawh]

I am filled with the healing light of wisdom and truth.

This mantra's sound brings healing to the bodymind, bringing relief from pain and suffering. It helps to remove the negative emotions of grief and hopelessness. It lifts the fear of change by developing awareness of the unchanging true self.

14. OM HRIM SHRIM DUM
[Om Hreem Shreem Doom]
I am powerful, fearless, and wise.

This mantra brings together the sounds that engender the inner resources of strength, courage, and intelligence to meet any challenge that comes your way.

15. LAM
[Luhm]
I am settled and secure.

Lam is the first of the six chakra mantras, which focus on the spiritual energy centers, or chakras, visualized along the spine. Its seed sound enlivens the first chakra, at the base of the spine, which connects us to our source of stability and security in life. It roots us securely in the earth, which stands for physical existence.

16. VAM
[Vuhm]
I am complete and content.

This mantra's seed sound enlivens the second chakra, located in the pelvic area. The second chakra is the energy center associated with creativity, sexuality, desire, and pleasure.

17. RAM

[Ruhm]

I am confidence and strength.

This mantra is the seed sound for the third chakra, located in the region of the solar plexus. It connects us to our source of strength and self-worth. You gain confidence and self-assurance at the level of the true self.

18. YAM

[Yuhm]

I am love and joy.

This mantra is the seed sound for enlivening the fourth, or heart, chakra, the space of feelings and emotions. When you can live in the present moment, the heart chakra is open to experience love and joy.

19. HAM

[Hum]

I am the expression of truth.

This mantra is the seed sound for enlivening the fifth, or throat, chakra, which is the center for speech and self-expression. When this chakra is open, your truth finds clear and complete expression in whatever you say and think. You are connected to the eternal truth of your true self.

20. KSHAM

[K'shum]

I am the light of pure knowing.

This mantra enlivens the sixth chakra, located between the eyebrows. Its seed sound connects you to the infinite knowledge of pure consciousness. When this energy center is activated, your thoughts, feelings, and actions are guided from within in an effortless flow.

21. PRAJNANAM BRAHMA

[Pruh-gyaw-num Brah-muh]

Consciousness is the wholeness of life.

This is a longer mantra that has a meaning. It is considered one of the great truths of existence. In this case the great truth is that everything is consciousness. In Sanskrit "everything" is Brahman, the One and All. Brahman is the ultimate reality. It is your source and the source of creation as a field of pure consciousness.

(If you find long mantras difficult to say, use the centering thought as your meditation.)

22. AYAM ATMA BRAHMA

[Ah-yum Aht-muh Brah-muh]

My essential nature is Brahman.

This mantra declares that each person's soul is united with everything in creation, or Brahman. Your soul, or Atman, is the most intimate part of you spiritually. There is a huge collection of separate people in the world, but every soul is actually an expression of wholeness. This gives everyone equal spiritual worth, which is infinite.

(If you find long mantras difficult to say, use the centering thought as your meditation.)

23. TAT TVAM ASI
[Tuht Tvum Ah-see]
I see pure awareness in everyone and everything.

This mantra means "You are That," where *That* refers to our spiritual essence. Call it the true self, pure consciousness, or Being, we share the same essence. The sound of this mantra enlivens your ability to see Being and essence in everyone equally. With that comes a total absence of judgment, while at the same time you see that in everyone there is boundless bliss at the level of the true self.

24. AHAM BRAHMASMI
[Uh-hum Brah-mah-smee]
I am Brahman.

This mantra means that the "I" (your true self) embraces everything in creation, or Brahman. In this declaration you affirm your spiritual wholeness. You bask in the light of pure awareness, which is your essence.

25. EKAM EVA DVITIYAM BRAHMA

[Eh-kuhm Eh-vuh Dvee-tee-yum Brah-mah]

Brahman is unity, without separation.

This mantra literally means that Brahman is the one reality, without a second. Therefore you are the one reality, too. No matter how separate, alone, or isolated you feel, wholeness has never lost sight of you. Pure consciousness awaits to support you in everything. Nothing has greater power than pure consciousness.

(If you find long mantras difficult to say, use the centering thought as your meditation.)

26. SO HAM

[So Hum]

I am.

This mantra is so simple that it is hard to see its real significance. "I am" means that your true self exists. It has never not existed. It will never cease to exist. Thus when you affirm "I am," you express nothing less than your eternal, immortal Being.

27. SARVAM KHALVIDAM BRAHMA

[Sahr-vum Kahl-vee-dum Brah-mah]

All this in truth is Brahman.

This mantra emphasizes that everything we experience, everything we think and feel—all of this—is the activity of pure consciousness. This is our eternal connection. From the viewpoint of your true self, the diversity of creation cannot hide the fact that everything (Brahman) comes from the same source. Pure consciousness is the womb of creation.

(If you find long mantras difficult to say, use the centering thought as your meditation.)

28. SAT CHIT EKAM BRAHMA
[Saht Chit Eh-kum Brah-mah]
Reality is one wholeness.

This mantra affirms that reality is whole. It isn't separated into inner and outer experiences. Rest assured that you are not separate and unseen. You are part of the wholeness, and your life is woven into the fabric of eternal existence.

(If you find long mantras difficult to say, use the centering thought as your meditation.)

29. OM TAT SAT
[Ohm Taht Saht]
Awareness embraces eternal truth.

This mantra affirms Truth with a capital T. To find this Truth, you have only to be aware. Your true self, being totally awake, knows only the truth. Because you exist here and now, you are the vehicle of eternal truth. Your life affirms the truth, and as you wake up, your truth becomes stronger and more powerful.

30. SATYAM SHIVAM SUNDARAM
[Saht-Yum Shee-vum Soon-dah-rum]
Pure existence is benevolent and beautiful.

This mantra affirms that awareness is the source of all that is good, true, and beautiful. These precious values are gifts from your very being. Your true self views your life as a flow of beauty and truth. By being awake, you stay in the flow all the time.

(If you find long mantras difficult to say, use the centering thought as your meditation.)

31. OM GAM GANESHAYA NAMAH
[Ohm Gum Guh-nesh-uh-yuh Nuh-mah]
I invite Nature's infinite intelligence.

This mantra invites the support of Nature into your life. Nature abounds in the creative intelligence of pure consciousness. Your true self was created to express every gift Nature has to offer. Here the gift is intelligence, which knows everything and can solve anything.

(If you find long mantras difficult to say, use the centering thought as your meditation.)

32. OM SHARAVANA BHAVAYA
[Ohm Shah-rah-vuh-nah Buh-vuh-yuh]
I invite the light of transformation.

You are surrounded by transformation and change, and this mantra invites personal transformation. In the gap between the ego and the true self, negative tendencies emerge. Pure consciousness can transform them completely. This mantra invokes the power of consciousness to accomplish any and all changes.

(If you find long mantras difficult to say, use the centering thought as your meditation.)

33. OM DUM DURGAYEI NAMAH
[Ohm Doom Dur-gah-yay Nuh-mah]
I invite the nurturing and protective power of my true self.

This mantra is about feeling safe and secure inside. By its nature, the ego is totally different from your true self. The ego feels unsafe, insecure, and defensive. In contrast, true self exists in total security, bringing you its nurturing and security. It alone can make you feel totally safe and secure.

(If you find long mantras difficult to say, use the centering thought as your meditation.)

34. OM TARE TUTTARE TURE SWAHA
[Ohm Tah-reh Too-tah-reh Too-rei Swa-ha]
I invite the support of everything necessary to me.

This mantra is about fulfilling your needs with the loving support of your true self. Where the ego struggles to fulfill a hodgepodge of needs, wishes, desires, and fantasies, your true self knows what you need to thrive and grow.

(If you find long mantras difficult to say, use the centering thought as your meditation.)

35. OM SAT CHIT ANANDA
[Ohm Saht Chit Ah-nahn-dah]
I invite eternal bliss consciousness.

This mantra affirms that your existence is unbounded bliss consciousness. Any happy experience is a taste of this bliss. No happiness is possible without it. As you wake up, bliss emerges simply by your being aware. Thus three things come together that can never perish: eternity, awareness, and bliss.

(If you find long mantras difficult to say, use the centering thought as your meditation.)

36. OM RAM RAMAYA SWAHA
[Ohm Rahm Rah-my-yah Swah-ha]
I invite the healing power of Nature.

This mantra activates the healing power of consciousness. The healing response is part of the design of the human body, and in meditation we extend this healing to the mind. Healing is part of Nature's design. Here you invite it to bring you physical, mental, and emotional healing.

(If you find long mantras difficult to say, use the centering thought as your meditation.)

37. OM NAMO NARAYANAYA
[Ohm Nah-moh Nah-rye-yah-nah-yah]
I invite balance and wholeness.

This mantra aligns you with Nature's power to balance mind and body. You return to your natural state of balance all the time, but some experiences can throw us into imbalances that hang on. This mantra invites consciousness to find these imbalances and correct them, whatever they are.

(If you find long mantras difficult to say, use the centering thought as your meditation.)

38. OM ARKAYA NAMAH
[Ohm Ark-eye-yah Nuh-mah]
I invite self-empowerment.

This mantra aligns your awareness with the infinite power of pure consciousness. Being whole, pure consciousness has nothing to fight against or protect itself from. Its power is absolute. With this mantra you invite the power and strength that only wholeness can bring.

(If you find long mantras difficult to say, use the centering thought as your meditation.)

39. OM MANGALAYA NAMAH
[Ohm Muhn-guh-lye-yah Nuh-mah]
I invite energy and passion.

Nature is infinitely dynamic and bursting with energy. This mantra invites energy into your life so that you can live it with passion. Passion is more than emotion. It expresses the infinite dynamism of pure consciousness coursing through you.

(If you find long mantras difficult to say, use the centering thought as your meditation.)

40. OM EIM SARASWATIYEI SWAHA

[Ohm I'm Sar-uh-swa-tee-yay Swa-ha]

I invite wisdom and inspiration.

This mantra activates your inner wisdom. Wisdom is more than knowledge or long experience. It embodies truth, applying it to everyday situations from a deep place inside you. This deep place is your true self. Here you invite it to give you the benefit of its wisdom.

(If you find long mantras difficult to say, use the centering thought as your meditation.)

41. OM SHRIM MAHA LAKSHIMIYEI NAMAH

[Ohm Shreem Mah-ha Lahk-shmee-yay Nuh-mah]

I invite abundance and prosperity.

This mantra is about the fullness of life. Nature abounds in all good things, and your true self connects you to the infinite abundance of pure consciousness. In your true self there is no feeling of lack. With this mantra you align with that viewpoint, overcoming any sense of lack you might have.

(If you find long mantras difficult to say, use the centering thought as your meditation.)

42. OM HRAUM MITRAYA NAMAH

[Ohm H'rouwm Mee-trah-yah Nuh-mah]

I connect myself with all of life.

Reverence of life is a perennial spiritual value. This mantra invites the energy that supports life wherever it arises. You are woven into the fabric of life, and the threads are loving and supportive. Just as pure consciousness supports you lovingly, you, too, can extend this support to life all around you.

(If you find long mantras difficult to say, use the centering thought as your meditation.)

43. OM GAM GURUBHYO NAMAH
[Ohm Gum Goo-roob-yo Nuh-mah]
I invite spiritual light into my heart.

This mantra lights the way on the path of awakening. There is incredible lightness in your being. When you carry this lightness in your heart, you walk the path with joy and optimism. Then the journeying itself brings fulfillment. There is no need to await the final goal, which is complete wakefulness. There is light and life in every moment of awakening.

(If you find long mantras difficult to say, use the centering thought as your meditation.)

44. OM SHRIM SHRIYEI NAMAH
[Ohm Shreem Shree-yeh Nuh-mah]
I open my awareness to total fulfillment.

This mantra invites complete inner fulfillment. The ego cannot know complete fulfillment or lead you to it. With this mantra, you amplify the qualities of success, abundance, beauty, love, and grace in every aspect of your life. Thus you learn that complete fulfillment isn't a far-off goal, but the very nature of your true self.

(If you find long mantras difficult to say, use the centering thought as your meditation.)

45. ARUL KARUNAI DAYA
[Ah -ruhl Ka-roon-eye Dah-yuh]
I invite loving kindness and empathy.

This mantra creates a space of compassion and acceptance in your heart. As compassion grows in the heart, your life becomes easier, more enjoyable, and blessed with grace and kindness.

(If you find long mantras difficult to say, use the centering thought as your meditation.)

46. OM NAMAH SHIVAYA
[Ohm Nuh-mah Shee-vah-yah]
I invite pure silence and transcendence.

Spiritual life goes beyond everyday life in the direction of pure silence, peace, and Being. To go beyond has been part of every spiritual path. What attracts us and keeps us going is the peace that passes all understanding existing deep inside of us. This mantra helps you deepen your inner silence so that transcending becomes natural and effortless.

47. SIDDHO HAM
[Sid-oh Hum]
I am awakened.

This mantra affirms that present awareness is always perfect, open, whole, and accepting. Nothing is missing or lacking in your Being. It asserts the truth that you are complete just as you are, right now. This truth is what gives you your value and necessary place in the universe.

48. NARASIMHA TAVADA SO HAM

[Nah-rawh-sim-ha Tah-vah-dah So Hum]

I am invincible awareness.

My consciousness transforms all negativity into its highest good. This mantra activates that aspect of our awareness that can transmute even the most intractable of problems into resolution and a useful evolutionary end.

(If you find long mantras difficult to say, use the centering thought as your meditation.)

49. SHRI DHANVANTRE NAMAH

[Shree Don-von-trey Nuh-mah]

I ask for healing of past hurts.

This mantra helps heal wounds and trauma from the past. Such hurts are too deep for the ego to reach. It fears returning to the pain of the past. But the true self heals without pain. There is nothing to probe or even think about. The healing power of consciousness works in silence with infinite care.

(If you find long mantras difficult to say, use the centering thought as your meditation.)

50. SHIVO HAM

[Shee-voh Hum]

In my essential nature I am divine.

This mantra means "I am divine," but the "I" in question isn't the ego. It is your true self, which is composed entirely of spirit. By aligning with the divine in yourself, you come closer and closer to the level of eternal Being. There you realize who you really are, and then there is no separation between the worldly and the divine.

51. AHAM PREMA
[Uh-hum Preh-mah]
I am love.

This mantra brings out another aspect of your true identity: You are love. With this knowledge you no longer have to pursue love. It is in your very nature. The love you receive from outside yourself is a reflection of your love. The more aware you are that you are love, the more you will see eternal love expressed in everything.

52. OM SHANTI OM
[Ohm Shahn-tee Ohm]
I radiate peace.

Shanti is the sound for peace in all its facets: peace in the mind, peace in the world, peace in existence itself. This mantra settles the emotional body and soothes the heart. It has the effect of calming any feelings of agitation and conflict. Repeating *Om Shanti Om* to yourself in meditation is a quiet affirmation that universal peace is your essential nature.

The Master Meditation

There are many ways to describe the state of complete awakening. One is said to dissolve like a drop in the infinite ocean or to radiate the light of life. In all directions all you can see is infinity. These are inspiring descriptions, but they have one fatal drawback. They try to express the inexpressible. This book was based on the notion that your mind is naturally capable of going into meditation. I thought that this one simple point had been missed by other meditation books, and it seemed to me to be a very profound point.

It is important to have a vision of your goal. Otherwise you cannot achieve it. If the goal of total meditation is to be completely awake, here and now, once and for all, can we envision it? I believe we can, through one final meditation. It's like a master meditation that includes all other meditations. In it, you don't disappear into the ocean of consciousness, but the opposite. You experience quite clearly that you are present everywhere, right this minute.

Unlike the previous meditations in this book, the master meditation has more than one step—there are seven, in fact—so you'll need 5 to 10 minutes to do the complete meditation.

THE MASTER MEDITATION

STEP 1: "I am present in everything I see."

Sit quietly with eyes closed and center yourself. Take 5 minutes to meditate on the following mantra: *Aham* (pronounced Ah-hum).

When you feel calm and settled, open your eyes but remain in your inner place. Let your eyes land on your surroundings without focusing on any particular object.

Say to yourself, "I am present in everything I see. Nothing is visible without me."

STEP 2: "I am present in everything I hear."

Close your eyes and remain centered. Now let the sounds in our surroundings come to you for a moment.

Say to yourself, "I am present in everything I hear. There is nothing to be heard without me."

STEP 3: "I am present in everything I touch."

With your eyes still closed, remain centered. Now let your fingers lightly touch your skin, clothing, and any object nearby like the chair you are sitting in.

Say to yourself, "I am present in everything I touch. There is nothing tangible without me."

STEP 4: "I am present in everything I taste."

With your eyes still closed, remain centered. Now taste the inside of your mouth. Mentally see a lemon being cut in half with a knife, spurting drops of juice. Taste the lemon's sourness.

Say to yourself, "I am present in everything I taste. Nothing has a taste without me."

STEP 5: "I am present in everything I smell."

With your eyes still closed, remain centered. Now gently inhale the smells in your surroundings; it doesn't matter what they are.

Say to yourself, "I am present in everything I smell. Nothing has an odor without me."

STEP 6: "I am present in everything I think."

With your eyes still closed, remain centered. Now let your mind go wherever it wants for a moment, to any random sensations, images, feelings, or thoughts. It doesn't matter what they happen to be.

Say to yourself, "I am present in everything I think. There is no mind without me."

STEP 7: "I am present everywhere."

With your eyes still closed, remain centered for the last step. Put your attention in the region of your heart. See invisible waves pulsing out from your heart in all directions. Follow them as far as you can until they fade away. For a moment expand how far the waves reach in all directions. It might help to envision the still surface of a pond. A raindrop strikes the surface, sending circular waves spreading out as far as the eye can see until they subside, and the pond is totally still once more.

Say to yourself, "I am present everywhere. Nothing can be without me."

To end the meditation, sit in the awareness of your being, which is silent, unmoving, unbounded, and present as the real you.

Once you have practiced it a few times, the master meditation is simple, but what does it mean? The meaning will change depending on your state of awareness. The goal is the same for everyone: to show you who you really are. It's good to have this exercise at hand, because we are constantly shifting our identity. You are no longer an infant, toddler, child, adolescent, or young adult. Those stages in life defined your ego as your personal story unfolded. Each stage was provisional; therefore, "I" was temporary, even though the ego likes to pretend that it is permanent and defines who you are.

Being a slave to change and impermanence, the ego can't really tell you who you are. You only begin to glimpse the truth when you notice that no matter how much your life changes, something remains constant. I call it the sense of self. Not many people pause in the busyness of their life to notice this silent companion. It has nothing to say, because your sense of self simply exists. It is your being. Words can only describe it as "I am."

"I am" doesn't sound like much. It doesn't participate in your personal story. "I" doesn't choose experience A and reject experience B. It has no likes or dislikes. You'd never expect that there's a secret hidden in "I am," but there is. Thanks to your sense of self, you are present everywhere. As you have found out in the master meditation.

You are present in everything you see. Try and see anything without being present—you can't. You cannot even imagine yourself not being present. Try to hear a sound without being present. Again, you can't. You went through the five senses and the mind (these are the six blind men in the Indian fable about the blind men and the elephant), and each shows you how present you are in every experience.

The reason the men are blind in the fable is that unless you experience wholeness—the elephant—the five senses and the mind cannot grasp reality. This is where Step 7 comes in. The waves spreading out in all directions are ripples in consciousness. The ripples rise and fall, and creation emerges in all its richness and magnificence. You are present in every aspect of reality that human beings are able to perceive. Try to imagine nonexistence. Try to imagine a time before you were born or a time after you die.

You will find these imaginings impossible, because you are merged into the elements that persist eternally. Time, space, matter, and energy exist for billions of years, but that isn't the same as eternity. Eternity consists of the two things that cannot change or be taken away: existence and consciousness. The real you is "I am," because those two little words express your existence and your awareness. Without a shadow of doubt, *you know that you are.*

The master meditation changes as you change. Most people, for example, will find it easy in Step 1 to grasp that they are present in everything they see. Photons, the carriers of light, are invisible. Light by itself isn't bright. It has no color. So unless you are present in everything you see, nothing can be seen. There aren't even light, colors, or pictures in the brain. It isn't the brain that is seeing; it is *you*.

As you wake up, this truth will become more intimate, personal, and powerful. There is room for the mind to stray. When you say to yourself, "Nothing is visible without me," your ego is bound to react. It will say, "Ridiculous. Of course the stars are visible without me. They existed for billions of years before I was born." But meditation has a way of sneaking around the ego. The next time you say to yourself, "Nothing is visible without me," your ego might not scoff. It might just hesitate and say, "Hmm."

So it will go, not in a straight line, but seemingly all over the place. You are being confronted with notions that baffle the ego, the limited, isolated, separate "I" you have identified with since birth. Fortunately, waking up is real. It makes you start to lose faith in the limited self. The day will come, perhaps very soon, perhaps over time, when you will say to yourself, "Nothing is visible without me," and you won't resist, hesitate, ponder, feel confused, or get distracted.

You will be struck with wonder. Imagine, all along you thought you were this tiny, insignificant "I," doing everything you can to feel secure, when all along you are the very essence of everything that can be seen. No matter how microscopic, you are the consciousness that makes seeing possible. No matter how cosmic, you are the essence that makes seeing possible. In a moment of wonder, the scales fall from your eyes, the conditioned mind lets go, and you silently merge with who you really are.

This is the summit of human experience. It has been around for all of recorded history. I love to explore the ins and outs of consciousness, because nothing is more fascinating than to unpack "I am" and discover that every discovery is contained inside it. But I am moved to wonder much more deeply by returning to the mystics and poets who have tongues to express ecstasy. They have gone beyond wonder to live in the bliss of eternal creation.

> Oh God
> I have discovered love!
> How marvelous, how good, how beautiful it is!
> I offer my salutation
> To the spirit of passion that aroused
> and excited this whole universe
> And all it contains.

That's the unmistakable voice of Rumi, but in the awakened life we will all speak with his voice. He opens a window to who we really are. The miracle, asleep as we are, is that we feel the truth when we meet it. A creation made out of love and passion sounds very human after all. It must, because we are the essence of creation, and we must never forget it.

ACKNOWLEDGMENTS

This book was completed in the dire months of the world-wide COVID-19 outbreak, and more than ever I feel grateful to those who have become my extended family. There is a personal connection and a bond of devotion with the Chopra Foundation and Chopra Global, my publisher, and most especially my long-time editor, Gary Jansen, who is remarkably fair and astute in our collaboration. Carolyn Rangel remains just as remarkable in her tireless devotion. Thanks to all of you from my heart. My wife, Rita, and I feel blessed to be surrounded by children and grandchildren who are just as precious to us now as the day they came into the world. May these bonds only strengthen as the world learns to heal again.

INDEX

happiness, 18, 55, 111, 267. *See also* bliss; joy

Hawkins, Gerald, 186

healing, 60–61, 63, 67, 85, 86. *See also* immune function
  healing mantras, 276–77, 290
  meeting discomfort or pain, 69–70, 229–30

The Healing Self (Chopra and Tanzi), 27

heart chakra, 278

heart development and function, 4, 5–6, 181–83

heart mantras, 276, 278

heart, nourishing and acting from, 242, 260. *See also* love

helplessness, 52–53, 109, 121

higher purpose and spirituality meditation, 257–62. *See also* spirituality

homeostasis, 41–42, 60

hopelessness, 109, 121

hormones, 63–64

Horton's syndrome, 76–77

human matrix, 154–62

humility, 247, 249, 262

"I am," 92–94, 281, 297–300

identity, 166–68, 264, 297

immune function, 60–61, 63, 83–84, 85. *See also* healing

impulsiveness and impulse control, 108, 111, 149, 154, 171, 172, 193–97

inner agendas, 187–89

inner knowing lesson, 35–37

inner silence, 219, 235–36, 247, 269–70, 289. *See also* quiet mind

insecurity, 234, 244, 249, 255, 284. *See also* safety and security

insight, 221–23, 225–28

insight meditations, 223–68
  asking for insight, 225–26
  Day 1: Safety and Security, 228–33
  Day 2: Success and Achievement, 233–39
  Day 3: Love and Bonding, 239–45
  Day 4: Personal Meaning and Value, 246–51
  Day 5: Creativity and Discovery, 251–57
  Day 6: Higher Purpose and Spirituality, 257–62
  Day 7: Wholeness and Unity, 263–68
  three questions to ask, 224–25
  what insights feel like, 226–28

intelligence, 82, 283. *See also* wisdom
  of the body, 60, 61
  of consciousness, 22, 23, 34, 272, 283

memory, 61–63, 83–84, 129–33
  discharging sticky emotions,
    141–43
  stickiness of past experiences,
    131–33, 135–41, 165–66
mental equilibrium (balance),
    40–41, 42–44, 47–48, 67
  restoring, 48–56
mind-body connection, 71–73. *See
    also* bodymind; disconnect/
    dissociation
mindfulness, 40, 48, 71, 185–89
miracle exercises, 201–17
  beauty, 205–6
  being, 216–17
  bliss, 214–15
  connection, 208–10
  light, 203–4
  love, 206–8
  revelation, 211–12
  transcendence, 213–14
  transformation, 204–5
  wakefulness, 210–11

Nature, 8, 10, 31, 56, 164, 283, 285
negative emotions and behaviors,
    88, 106, 108–13, 171. *See
    also* emotions; stuckness
    syndrome; *specific emotions*
  coexistence of opposite
    emotions, 190
  dealing with negative emotions,
    64–67

discharging sticky emotions,
    141–43
easiest ways to wake up,
    179–80
habits lesson, 114–19
noticing lesson, 185–89
not "in here," not "out there"
    lesson, 29–30

obsessive-compulsive disorder
    (OCD), 115
obstacles. *See* difficult situations;
    insight meditations;
    resistance; self-empowerment
ocean analogies, 89, 100, 101, 148,
    160–62
oneness. *See* wholeness and unity

pain, meeting and coping with,
    69–70, 76–78, 79, 229–30
parenting, 173–74, 188. *See also*
    children and adolescents
passion mantra, 286
past experiences. *See* memory;
    sticky memories/experiences;
    stuckness syndrome
peace mantra, 291
peak experiences, 79–80, 195
penicillin, 186, 188
perception. *See* sensation/
    perception
personal meaning and value, 220,
    246–51

self-doubt, 152–53, 266
self-empowerment, 145–68
  basics, 145–46
  drawing on hidden powers,
    165–68
  and ego, 151, 152–54
  the human matrix, 154–62
  least effort lesson, 147–50
  mantra for, 286
  oneness lesson, 163–65
self-esteem and self-worth, 108, 166,
    220, 246–51
self-inquiry, 40, 48–49, 137–38, 140,
    151–52, 254–55. *See also* insight
    meditations
self-judgment, 108, 167–68, 245,
    262, 267
sensation/perception, 36–37, 159, 176,
    179. *See also* miracle exercises
  incorporating into master
    meditation, 295–96
  mental vs. physical, 29–30
  and the mind-body connection,
    71, 92–93
  of total awareness, 78–79
  what insights feel like, 226–28
sexuality, 97–98, 243, 244, 277
shabda, 270
Shakespeare, William, 97–98
shame, 97–98, 108, 115, 166, 195
shock, 76
silence, 269–70. *See also* inner
    silence

sleep, 90
slime molds, 22–24
solar plexus chakra, 278
Sonnet 129 (Shakespeare), 97–98
spirituality, 13, 18, 53, 71, 175, 220,
    240. *See also* prayer
  and awareness, 17, 78, 228
  and detachment, 11, 76
  and evil, 105, 106, 110
  higher purpose and spirituality
    meditation, 257–62
spiritual mantras, 273, 287–88,
    289
spontaneity lesson, 193–97
sticky memories/experiences,
    131–43. *See also* stuckness
    syndrome
  discharging sticky emotions, 134,
    141–43
  and emotional charge, 131, 135,
    140
  stickiness lesson, 135–43
Stonehenge, 186
strength mantras, 275, 277
stress, xv, 54, 87–89, 111. *See
    also* anxiety; difficult
    situations
  as awareness trigger, 78–79
  controlled breathing for,
    54–55
  examining areas of, 232–33
  physical stress responses, 86,
    87–88

stuckness syndrome, 106, 107–10,
    121–23, 125. *See also* resistance;
    sticky memories/experiences
    freeing yourself of sticky
        emotions, 134, 141–43
    getting unstuck, 106–7, 111–13,
        123, 135, 168, 179–81
    habits lesson, 114–19
success and achievement, 220,
    233–39
suffering, 55, 107, 111
"Surprised by Joy" (Wordsworth),
    215
sweat lodge ceremonies, 77
synchronicity, 208–10

talent, 131, 132, 133
Tanzi, Rudolph, 27
testosterone, 63–64
Thích Nhất Hạnh, xix, xx
third-eye chakra, 279
Thoreau, Henry David, 16–17
thoughts and thinking. *See also*
    contemplation; decision
    making; judgment; memory;
    rationality; reflection
    and anxiety, 64–67
    and awareness, 5, 6, 43, 165–66
    dismissing negative thoughts, 117
    getting out of thinking mode,
        118
    and meditation, 44, 67–68
    meeting painful thoughts, 69–70

thinking before speaking or
    making a decision, 171, 172
thoughts as revelations, 211–12
transformational thinking,
    98–99
vs. feeling, 81–83
zero point lesson, 45–47
throat chakra, 278
total meditation. *See also* insight
    meditations; mantra
    meditations; master
    meditation; total meditation
    as exploration of consciousness,
        10, 11, 28, 37, 39, 43
    key features and benefits of,
        10–12, 15, 16, 17–19, 24, 139–40
transcendence exercise, 213–14
transformation, 5, 80, 174, 175–77,
    204–5, 283–84
trauma, 78–79, 133–34, 290. *See also*
    healing
truth, 223, 224–25, 246, 254, 283
    truth mantras, 273, 276–77, 278,
        282, 287

unbounded lesson, 101–2
unbounded mantra, 276
uncertainty/predictability, 189–92
unconditional love, 239–41
unconsciousness, 170, 171, 174,
    179. *See also* awareness;
    mindfulness
unity. *See* wholeness and unity

ABOUT THE AUTHOR

DEEPAK CHOPRA, MD, FACP, founder of the Chopra Foundation, a nonprofit entity for research on well-being and humanitarianism, and Chopra Global, a modern-day health company at the intersection of science and spirituality, is a world-renowned pioneer in integrative medicine and personal transformation. Dr. Chopra is a clinical professor of family medicine and public health at the University of California, San Diego, and serves as a senior scientist with Gallup Organization. He is the author of more than eighty-nine books translated into over forty-three languages, including numerous *New York Times* bestsellers. His ninetieth book and national bestseller, *Metahuman: Unleashing Your Infinite Potential* (Harmony Books), unlocks the secrets to moving beyond our present limitations to access a field of infinite possibilities. *Time* magazine has described Dr. Chopra as "one of the top 100 heroes and icons of the century."